A TALE OF THREE CITIES

Reno, Carson, San Francisco; 1863-1930

The Saga and Humor of an Old Pioneer Family

by

Bertha Bender Brown

Edited by Vinson Brown

Copyright 1964, Naturegraph Company

LC 65-690

Published by Naturegraph Company
Healdsburg, California

TABLE OF CONTENTS

FOREWORD 3

FATHER AND MOTHER 4

GIRLHOOD AND GIRLHOOD FRIENDS . . . 28

SERVANTS OF THE FAMILY 45

STORIES OF UNCLE HENRY YERINGTON . 55

STORIES ABOUT DR. BROWN 71

SAN FRANCISCO TO LOS ANGELES BY BIKE . 76

SAN FRANCISCO AND THE EARTHQUAKE . . 85

FOREWORD

By Vinson Brown

My mother, the author of this book, passed away on July 16, 1962, almost exactly 84 years after she was born so long ago in the newly named little town of Reno. She used to tell me that, before Reno was named in 1877, it was called "the dirty little town on the Truckee!" But I am sure she was as proud of her home town as anybody could be, though I am not sure she approved of all of its recent developments. Since I was born in Reno too, and share with her a common love for this place that has also been called "the City of Trembling Leaves," it is with a great deal of pleasure that I have been able to bring this book of hers to the attention of the public. I am only very sorry that she was unable to see it in print before she died.

There is much nostalgia in these pages and also much savory humor. For those who are still alive who lived in the times and places spoken about by my mother, this book will bring back many fond memories. For those too young to know of these things, it will perhaps help give a clearer picture of the times and doings of their own ancestors and the common hopes and dreams that have made life more interesting for all of mankind down through the ages.

My mother was a very human person, with some of the faults most of us have. But I will remember her best as one whose love and guidance surrounded me like a great warm blanket when I was a child, and whose story here also shows her in her own glorious youth when there was magic in everything about her, from her kind and dignified, but sometimes comical, father, to the inconsequential in the long run, but vastly important at the time, tragedies of her girlhood. May she live as long in your memories as she does in mine!

In June 19, 1868, the tough work in solid rock above Donner Lake and above Truckee was completed and in June the Central Pacific Railroad was completed through to Reno, the tough little town by the Truckee, or, as it is called now, "The Biggest Little City in the World."

To Reno is where my father came to open the telegraph office for the Central Pacific, a job he obtained through the influence of his uncle, Edwin B. Crocker, who was closely associated with that railroad. He had earlier been a telegrapher at Virginia City, where he had arrived by covered wagon in 1863 at the age of nine.

My father, as a boy , had difficulty in carrying a tune and left school when his teacher tried to force him to sing. His uncle later placed him in some special school to be taught telegraphy. There he worked and studied until he won, at the age of 21, a $5,000 lottery prize. With this, he then went to San Francisco and took a course in banking at Heald Business College.

When he returned to Reno, he was ready, with others who were interested, to open the first independent bank in the state of Nevada. This became the Washoe County Bank. He was cashier and manager of that bank for forty-four years, at the end of which time he actually died in harness, sitting in the chair in which he began.

My father's two older brothers, Wilse and Almon, came across the country in covered wagons in 1862 in response to the Comstock boom at Virginia City. They sold papers on the streets of that famous mining camp and, when they had money enough, sent for the family. The father, Jacob Bender, was an expert tailor and had hopes of opening a shop to support his family. But he soon died, leaving his wife and three boys and three girls.

The family then went for awhile to Sacramento to live near Aunt Margaret, my grandmother's oldest sister, and her husband, Judge Edwin Crocker.   He was a brother of Charles Crocker, one of the "Big Four" who financed the building of the Central Pacific Railroad. Judge Crocker was the lawyer who conducted all the legal work for the railroad in Sacramento and in Washington.   He was a highly educated man and became a prominent judge in Sacramento, making his home also in Washington, and later in San Francisco.

My father was in Reno in 1876 when he met my mother.   She was born on a farm near Elmira, New York, and was one of the first graduates of the Elmira College for Women.   She was gifted with a very pleasing voice and came out to Reno to visit cousins by the name of Hatch.   She was soon having a very gay time and met my father at a party.   He became very interested in her, but was too shy to pop the question.   So he wrote his proposal on paper, came into the room where she was and threw it at her, immediately beating it out of the room.   She had to run after him to give him her answer!

Between the families, there were many who planned to go back by train to Elmira, where it was decided to have the wedding.   So father's Aunt Margaret Crocker provided a private train to hold all the relatives.   Her daughter, Jennie, went along and, when she got off the train in Elmira, she met Mother's cousin, J. Sloat. Fassett.   He knew at once she was the right girl for him.   When told that she was very rich, he exclaimed, "Well, that's all right; I'll just make as much as she has!"   This he actually did later through his experience and interests in mining and in shipping mahogany out of the Philippines. He even once sent my mother's brother, Charles Fassett there to set up a mill for him. It was shipped from San Francisco, set up in sections and Uncle Charley went along to get it all going right.

Uncle Charley Fassett was Mother's only brother. Having lost the sight of one eye as a boy, his education suffered, but that didn't stop him, as, through correspondence courses and his work, he became a successful mining man, living mostly in Spokane, Washington. Later he became Mayor of Spokane, using a fine violin he had to charm his audiences when campaigning. This violin is now being used by my granddaughter, Tamara.

On their way to the wedding, the party in the private railroad car stopped in Philadelphia to visit the 1776-1876 Centennial Exposition or World's Fair, which was about to close. Many of the wedding presents were bought at this Fair, and now the former Bender children all have choice pieces from it in their homes. Florence had the silver in Paisley pattern given her, a pattern still on sale at Tiffanys in New York City, and also has a very beautiful cameo set. I have a bronze deer, standing three feet high, and very handsome. Homer has a gold clock, and so forth.

In the first ten years of Reno's existence, Clara and I were born, she in 1877 and I in 1878. This was a rugged time in Reno, and not far from our home a man was hanged by vigilantes in 1877. To provide a home for his new family, Father bought an auctioned-off lot on what afterward turned out to be the wrong side of the tracks. He must have bought the acre and the home the first year of marriage, and later not only added rooms but also an extra acre on the next block, which was used for pasture for two cows, horses and chickens. This home still stands on Ralston near Third Street.

Some other acres Mother's cousins, the Hatch family, decided to sell, and offered to Father for five thousand dollars. It included a home on the court house square and the land extended back for many acres on Virginia Road, including property now worth in the millions! Father unfortunately did not have the money.

It is remarkable that Father got his start as a banker by gambling on a lottery and winning the grand prize,
but never gambled again. He felt he must set a good
example to his employees. He would never bet on a horse
race and felt very sure that gambling, tied in with cig-
arette smoking, were evils. He smoked cigars, which
he considered fit for a man, and sometimes tried an
evil-smelling pipe, over his children's objections.

One older brother of father's, David Almon Bender,
married a girl in Sacramento and lived in Carson City,
Nevada.   He was Land Agent for the Virginia   and
Truckee Railroad. Next to his home, he and his brothers built a small cottage for their mother.

D. A. , as this brother was called, was a great talker, but he was very interesting and fascinated us with
tales of his life in Virginia City.   Unfortunately, all of
those tales are gone from my memory.   The only one
my father used to tell his boys was about how he rode a
sled with his friends from the upper slopes of Mt. Da-
vidson down the very steep Virginia City hills, seeing
how many narrow escapes they could have by sledding
between the big wheels of the giant ore wagons, and also racing a mile or more farther down into a deep can-
yon! I guess boys are still the same in all ages and
times because my son has tried similar wild stunts.

Before Uncle Almon had his mother living near him
in Carson City, he had his youngest sister Clara, after
whom my oldest sister was named, up for a visit.   She
was then wooed and won by the very big catch and wid-
ower of the town, Henry Marvin Yerington, the famous
Superintendent of the Virginia and Truckee Railroad.
He had four children, the oldest being the same age as
Clara was, and right here I want to say that the many
writers about the early Comstock days of the V. and T.
Railroad all missed a big chance to write about a man

who was the most colorful figure of all that time, Henry M. Yerington. I will have more to say about him later.

Though many nice visitors came to see us in Reno, some proved not so nice. They usually came from the East, and had fine letters of introduction as sons of wealthy bankers or insurance men, and the letters usually said, "I would appreciate it very much, any kindness and attention you can give my son, who will be a stranger in your midst." Poor Father! He would ask them to dinner and take them for a ride and then be completely taken in himself by the fine line each would hand him. But many turned out to be scamps, who borrowed money that they never intended to return, men whose families were well rid of them in the East. Father learned from sad experience to be very careful.

But with many poor people in Reno he was very helpful. When he passed to the beyond, one of the people telling of his help was a Chinese laundryman, who couldn't meet his payroll at times. My father constantly helped him in his hours of need, and was always repaid in cash as well as in deed. At one time the Chinaman was loaded with laundry for some family up the river, which was covered with ice that day, and saw my younger brother, Edwin, trying to skate. He stopped to watch him, and fortunately was there to see him fall through a weak place in the ice. The Chinaman dropped his basket of clothes and waded into the ice-cold river. He got hold of Edwin and pulled him out, delivering him home wrapped in his own coat.

Early in Father's life in the bank he kept getting colds so constantly that he felt this was due to his bald head and went down below (San Francisco), to buy himself two toupees. Of course all the children who knew him teased him a lot about it. Well, one day he had the three-seated buckboard hitched up to take his daughters

Charles T. Bender as a young man

Julia Fassett Bender with second child, Bertha

1854 1904

"At Evening time there shall be light."

Samuel Montague Fassett
Grandfather Fassett

Ruth Marvin Fassett
Grandmother Fassett

Charles and Julia Bender, with daughter Florence and
grandaughter Elizabeth

Uncle Charlie Fassett   Julia Fassett Bender
About 1880   About 1920

and their little girl friends for a ride. This often happened and, before he arrived home from the bank, they would be lined up waiting for him. Mother would often protest that she never had a chance for a ride herself when that wagon was out at the post waiting!

Anyway, off we started, with Father singing his favorite tune, "Old Dog Tray," which was about the only one he ever used. This time we all drove out east of Reno towards Sparks where the big railroad shops were and just below which was an old wooden bridge that crossed the Truckee. There also we found quite a breeze blowing and, unfortunately, Father took off his cap for some reason as one of the stronger gusts came along. The wind merrily lifted his toupee off his head and sailed it right down into the middle of the river! But we children thought this was the best joke ever and were sent off into gales of laughter, giggling about the mishap all the way home!

Another funny ride Father took was when he bought the big new car, one of the first ones in Reno, but only Mother was his passenger that day. They took to the back roads to get away from traffic and crowds. Suddenly a cow showed up right in the middle of the road, but Father kept right on going, knocking the cow over! Fortunately the animal was not badly hurt, but Mother was greatly incensed at his carelessness and cried:

"Didn't you see that cow?"

"Sure I did!" he snapped back, "but the cow saw me first! So she should have got out of my way!"

Mother was a clever story teller and remembered so many of the funny things that happened in our lives.

I doubt if a father ever lived who cared so much for little girls and was so kind to them. Once, when he was taking a visitor out for a drive, many little girls waved at him, as he went by, calling, "Hello, Daddy Long Legs!" which was their nickname for him. Finally the visitor exclaimed:

"Mr. Bender, you told me you had six children, but I am sure I have counted many more than that!"

Father had one beautiful horse given to him by Governor Sparks. He was bred for racing but, in some way, did not come up to the right points that counted for a good racer. So this handsome brown horse, Granger, became the most beloved of all our possessions. He was very high-spirited, especially when hitched to a single buggy, as he seemed to know he was showing off before the whole town, and put on a most spectacular display of prancing, pacing and tossing his head when he knew he had a stranger in the rig.

He would be hitched up and seemed to know all about what was going to happen. The minute Father came around the corner, turning towards home, Granger would begin to paw the dirt and whinny and snort. After showing off to the town, with Granger shying in imitation fear at every odd thing along the road, or marching along with his head so proud and high, they would finally cross the Virginia Street Bridge, and then Granger would tremble all over and put his head down and wait for the signal Father would give.

"Go!" Father would shout, and off our noble horse rushed, faster than a Nevada Zephyr. My how he loved that race, passing everything on the road, and Father loved it just as much!

But, other times, when he was hitched up to the family phaeton, with Mother taking we children along, he would know he had to go slow and would just hang his head down, as if he were an old plug. It would make

Mother so provoked! But even the whip would not make him change his pace or posture. It was as if he were saying:

"I'm made for splitting the wind, not this kind of family go slow stuff!" But, nevertheless, he would take us in the phaeton as if all the responsibility were on his shoulders and he must see that not even the smallest child fell off!

Men about town knew that Granger was broken to ride, and there was seldom a parade coming up that someone would not go into the bank and beg of Father to let him ride Granger. Father would usually say:

"I don't allow anybody to ride him."

But they always knew better and would promise nothing would happen to them until Father broke down and loaned Granger to the asker. Yet no one ever lasted out the ride. Granger would take them calmly enough until they felt safe, and then, usually when crossing the railroad tracks, he would just as calmly dump the rider on the ground and run for home!

Mother's parents sold their farm in Elmira, New York, and moved first to Reno. Grandfather Fassett I thought very quiet and lovable, but Grandma was sure she could make me into a good Baptist like herself. I was taken by her one day to see a funeral of a young lady friend of mine whom Grandma claimed was going to heaven because she was a good Baptist like herself. I took one look at the corpse, let out a yell that could be heard for blocks, and ran all the way home. Mother put the kibosh on Grandma's proselyting after that!

On my grandfather Fassetts side his ancestors went back to England. He rarely spoke of such things, but once jokingly told one granddaughter that if she cared to follow back the Montague ancestory of his family, she would be surprised at what she would find, maybe a pirate or two! I agreed also with one cousin of mine, who was hunting back through the Bender ancestory, and finally stopped her search, saying:

"If I go to the next generation, I know I will find they stole sheep!"

This cousin, Margaret Bender, was sometimes held up to me by my father as an example of what not to do, as she was a great favorite of Aunt Margaret Crocker, and was often taken on costly trips to Europe, and given an elaborate life, until Father was sure she was very spoiled! I didn't agree, as I was envious of those trips, but Father felt that Reno could give us all we needed in life. He fought against my older brother, Homer, going to Boston Tech for his education, but Homer courageously worked long enough to get money for his books and fare east and just left. Then Father came forth resignedly to help him.

There was never a man more loyal to Nevada or more willing to help worthy people start new businesses there than my Father. When people he trusted needed money and couldn't get a loan from the bank, Father would put his hand in his own pocket to help them. I believe he never was disappointed in these people and we know of one man, who once had the finest shoe repair shop we have ever seen in Reno, who was helped by him in that way. One poor woman was struggling with a few acres, raising pigs in the eastern part of the valley. She wanted to educate her son but didn't have the money or security. Father put his trust in her and her son was educated and later became a United States Senator from Nevada, Patrick McCarran.

Long before we got our first phone, Father decided to put in a private telegraph wire from the bank to our home so Mother could call him in any emergency. He carefully taught her, he thought, how to use the key to tap out her messages. However, it did not always work out that way, and one day she thought she had sent a clear message for him to meet the noon train from Carson, as his sister Flora was coming for a visit. He fortunately happened to have the horse and carriage down town, having Granger, our horse, shod that day.

We were all waiting and ready at lunch time for Father to come with Aunt Flora. But, instead, Father arrived alone and very much upset.

"Why the dickens, " he demanded, "did you send me a message to buy another sack of potatoes when you know we have plenty of potatoes out in the store room? Why should I bring home another sack? Why? Why?"

I remember he was very red in the face, but he got a good deal redder when Mother finally got a word in edgewise to demand in her turn:

"Well, I never ordered you to get any potatoes, but where is Aunt Flora whom I told you to pick up at the station? What about her?"

"I don't know what you're talking about!" Father roared.

At last it became clear that Mother had mixed up her message on the telegraph and I do not think Father was ever sure again about any message she sent. As for we children, we had a most terrible time keeping straight faces that day!

Mother loved to entertain, especially one group who were all good story tellers, as Mother was. There usually were twelve altogether and one was the Episcopal Minister. He was a Rev. Jenvey, and he was small and fat and very jolly, but in those times ministers were not supposed to have much humor as they usually took life quite seriously.

One evening, when the Reverend Jenvey came for dinner at our place, Mother asked him to say "Grace." We were used to long and drawn out prayers from ministers at such times, so some of the family I am sure were praying that he would not be too long, as we were hungry. He surely answered our prayers, for he looked up suddenly to ask Mother:

"Mrs. Bender, are there any ministers present?"

"No," she answered, "there are no others," which he well knew.

Reverend Jenvey bowed his head once more and said with great solemnity:

"Well then, let us thank God!" And that was our Grace that night!

One time Father got the bright idea that he would like to take his family to live in the country. Knowing that one ranch, about five miles east of Reno, was for sale, he broached the subject, but Mother wasn't pleased. I believe she was especially not pleased because this happened just after Father had to sell or dispose of Edwin's pony because he was racing it through the town too much. However, Father insisted on taking us all down to see the ranch and I am sure we children, at least, were all thrilled at the prospect.

Mother didn't say a word until she saw the kitchen wood box. It was really a built-on room, with one window facing the yard where wood could be thrown in and the other window opening into the kitchen. Mother asked who was to bring in the wood. There was silence

from the two boys, Edwin and Homer, as they didn't
like the job at home and always fought about whose turn
it was. Then she thought of something else. She pictured herself in vivid detail balancing herself on the
edge of the middle window and trying to reach down for
the last sticks of wood! That was too much for Father
and he never said another word about buying that farm!
Mother used to make the most of this story and could
start everybody laughing, but it did not amuse Father.

Father's family were all Episcopalians, but he seldom went to church himself, as he felt that Sunday was
the one day off he had to give to his children. As long
as the weather was good, we were taken on long rides
and picnics. He had a special three-seated wagon and
two horses for such trips. He felt there were too many
men going to church to show off their piety, who practiced shady deals in their businesses during the week.
I believe we had more love and respect for our father
than most children did and certainly more companion-
ship with him. I was the one who could get up early on
Sunday mornings and fix the lunches, so I was his
"picnic girl." he said. The rest all loved to sleep late.
But, by nine-thirty we'd be off and away on a merry
trip, often with other children with us.

Mother was much more religious, at least on the
surface, than father, but she had her fingers in so many
religious and social pies that she sometimes confused
us, though, no doubt, she was one of the most stimu-
lating members of the Reno community as a whole.
Thus, she put on the first home talent play with many
local people struggling to act for the first time. She
sang most beautifully in the Episcopal Choir, but turned
right around and started the first Unitarian Church in
Reno, even acting as minister! She even went looking
for outside talent for our schools and brought the well-

known Professor Billinghurst to Reno to be Superintendent of Schools.

Sometimes the eastern newspapers in particular
would like to poke fun at the state of Nevada and her
wild ways, and this would always disgust mother, who
liked to think of Reno becoming more and more sophis-
ticated and urbane under her guidance.   She became
really outraged when they published a story about the
"highlight" of Reno society being a corner saloon on
First Street across from the railroad depot. This saloon widely advertised that it was being made over with
most beautiful decorations and appointments and that
its opening night would see it attended by all the society people in Reno.   The eastern papers took up the
story as if it were seriously true and played it for all
it was worth!

It so happened that Mother had a cousin in Elmira,
New York, who was a strong member of their Baptist
Church, and he evidently saw the article picturing this
saloon as the show place of Nevada society. He took it
for granted, for some reason, that Mother would, of
course, be there for the grand opening, and he wrote
her a letter, asking her to give him a description of
the affair and how she was dressed and so forth. Mother was so astonished and so mad that she didn't write
for days, but, when she did, I'll wager he took a real
beating!

In writing my memories, my thoughts continually go
back to my father, and his constant wish to take his
pleasure with his family when we were young and grow-
ing up. I went on many trips with him into the country,
either on our bycycles or by team and wagon. He lived
only long enough to enjoy two of his grandchildren,
Marvin Humphrey and Elizabeth Carpenter. Whether
they remember his lovable ways I don't know, but I re-

ather, Charles T. Bender   Mother, Julia Fassett Bender

ld Bender Family home on Ralston Street in Reno.

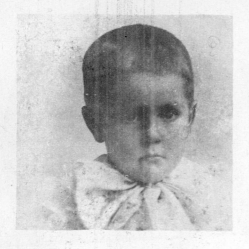

Edwin S. Bender, age 4

Homer C. Bender, age 1(

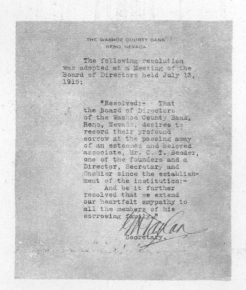

Resolution of Washoe Co. Bank

Kate, age one, with
cousin of her mother,
Elmira, N. Y.,

member his constant need and love for Marvin, the first grandchild, and then for Elizabeth. Of course they did not grow big enough while he was still alive for him to take them on trips, as he did us, and perhaps he was getting too old. Also his last days were clouded with sorrow by the loss of his oldest daughter, Clara Louise, which was a terrible blow to him from which he never recovered.

He had another blow during his life that meant both terrible worry and sorrow and no doubt directly helped bring on his death from diabetes.

During the boom days of Goldfield and Tonopah, big mining camps in southern Nevada, and also in similar mining boom towns, fortunes were wildly won and wildly lost, and men often took chances who would never gamble in other ways. Father's position for all the years of his business life had been without a flaw, but, through his brother Almon, he was persuaded to join a group of fine men in Carson who were starting in branch banking out through the mining camps. Unfortunately, the man who was put in charge of the branches out at these places was a Mr. T. B. Rickey, and he was later found to have made many bad loans. When Father and the other men in Carson found out what was going on, they tried to stop it, but could do nothing.

Time and again Father tried to resign from the board of directors, as the bank records show, but the other men were not willing to give up his leadership, knowing that if anybody could save them he could. But Rickey wouldn't listen to him or the rest and the whole venture finally failed, while Rickey fled the state and the other men stayed to pay up the loss.

Father immediately resigned from his own bank in Reno, where his record was flawless, but the directors refused his resignation and the townspeople stood back of him 100%. But it was a very great blow to him and, not many years after this, he developed the illness that took him from us.

One night he and Mother took the train to San Francisco. He went to the smoking compartment for his last night's cigar, and then didn't come back for so long that Mother became worried. Finally he returned, but was as pale as a sheet and almost fell into a faint. He finally said:

"Well! At last I had the chance to meet Rickey face to face, and I certainly told him what I thought of him. That he took all the directors down to a terrible loss didn't matter to him!"

Father's brother, Almon, who was instrumental in getting the two men from Reno to take his part, was stricken with strokes and lay paralyzed for years. He had promised to cover Father's losses, but could only murmur, "no money, no money!"

Father often made business trips to the City (San Francisco), and would register at the Palace Hotel. Almost invariably a man would call him up on the phone and ask.

"Are you my long lost brudder, Charley?"

Whether Father ever convinced him he was not, I do not know, but it happened quite often.

Once, when he went to the City on business, he decided to bring Mother a present and asked the advice of a friend. She was the wife of a sea captain, and a fine person, but with a different taste than Mother's. She insisted that he buy his wife a hat, and said she would get it herself. Well, he arrived with the hat box and

Mother was not only surprised, but paralyzed! It was very large and colorful, but about as suitable for Mother as a flower crown would be for Father. But she had a hard time convincing Father that he never again should buy her a hat, as he was sure it was quite beautiful!

Mother was leader of a Choral Society or group of singers, and they took part in many benefit shows in Reno, but she never dreamed of being serenaded by the group herself. However, when her first boy child was born, early one Christmas morning, the carollers were outside in the snow, singing "Hail to the New Born King."

Here are Mother's own notes on some of the things she took part in during those early days in Reno:

"Yes, I sang at everything and taught school under Professor Orvis Ring for a short time (he who has a school named after him in Reno). I was offered $100 a month and my board to go out to Cherry Creek to teach two pupils and it was a nice rich bachelor (widower?) who made the offer! (She was not married at this time.) At the old Reno Theatre, where Dromiacks Hotel now stands, I put on the first play that was ever given in Reno. It was called 'Down by the Sea.' The story was about two sons who were adopted by an old sea captain and named 'March and September Gale' because they were born during those months, each after a big storm that threw up ship wrecks on the shore. Charlie Fassett, my brother, was September Gale and Joe Dillman was March Gale.

"I helped start the first kindergarten and Papa and I were instrumental in opening the first public library in Reno. Gertrude Shoemaker was the first librarian, and, for months, I collected the money to pay her, and the rent. No one gave over one dollar a month and most only 50¢. We paid $30.00 rent a month, and paid her $30.00 a month wages. The building was on the corner of Sierra and Commercial Row, opposite Mr. Eaton's hardware store."

In the old days in Reno the people had to provide most of their own amusements, so a Nevada Club was formed and a club house built. It had a room for cards downstairs and another room for dancing upstairs. Every family entertained once a year, with each hostess providing the refreshments of her own choice. Card parties and dancing alternated each week. Father loved to play cards, but he did learn to dance finally.

Mother happened to be famous for her doughnuts and we usually served them with coffee and cider. But mother was also known for her saltrising bread, and she could always expect calls by phone asking if she would serve doughnuts or saltrising bread for some afternoon party. So far as I know, this club is still in operation in Reno.

Father also joined the Sierra Club of California, being one of the first members, and one of his funniest stories is about a trip he and another member, with some also from California made up through the Sierras. They packed their food along and expected to have a royal time, which they did, but not in the way expected!

You see, Mother's dearest friend was a Mrs. Josephine Jones, who lived in a house directly opposite the Reno Court House. Mrs. Jones was a real southerner and always served her famous beaten southern biscuits at her dinners. One of their special attractions was that they stayed fresh longer than any other biscuit. So Mother got full directions as to how to make these biscuits for the Sierra campers and Father talked to the rest of the campers considerably about the treat they could look forward to!

Sad to say, however, the baking was somehow not done right and even the first day of the camp the biscuits came out hard as bricks! All the men tried and tried, but could get hardly a bite off of one. Around the campfire a few goats had gathered, hoping for some left-over food. So the men began to throw the biscuits at them and the goats tried their best to eat them. But nothing doing! So the goats tried extra hard and, suddenly, one biscuit shot out of the jaws of one goat all slippery with saliva. Well sir, all those goats just went wild over those biscuits then and started a regular circus, with biscuits shooting in all directions!

The men laughed so hard they couldn't eat, but just rolled helplessly on the ground. They never forgot that story of Charley's biscuits and the shooting goats and it spread all over town. For many years it was one of the funny stores in our home, but usually our mother was not too pleased when the subject was brought up!

When Father died it was typical of his indomitable spirit that he went into a coma in his office chair at the bank, surrounded by his work, and with his two sons, Homer and Edwin, working there with him. They carried him gently home and there he passed peacefully away.

Word was sent immediately to John Mendall in San Francisco. He was on the board of one of the large insurance companies and idolized Father. He grabbed his hat and caught the first train to Reno where he took charge of all the arrangements for the body to be taken to San Francisco for cremation. He always said that he gave Father all the credit for his rise from errand boy to the top of the ladder in insurance. He was often in Reno and always stayed at our home and had a great trust in Father's judgment and advice. Once he came to Reno with his bride, who was very attractive, with

beautiful reddish hair.   She was hoping to make a fine
impression on all of us, but the wood and coal engines
used in those days for pulling trains over Donner Summit made this impossible and she arrived a sorry sight
indeed, her face covered with soot and her hair black!
During the many years later, when I was in touch with
her in Berkeley, we often laughed over that time of her
downfall!

Father's body was cremated in San Francisco, and
then his ashes were put into a copper urn and taken by
his sons to the Nevada side of Lake Tahoe where they
were dropped into the depths of that beautiful lake, as
were Mother's ashes much later.   This was Father's
wish, as he was so loyal to Nevada and all she had given
him that he never wanted to leave that state, even in
death.   Our sister Clara was also cremated, but her
husband, Frank Humphrey, wanted her ahses buried in
the Reno burial grounds where her sons would know she
rested and would be reminded each year of the mother
they lost.

The following tribute was paid my father, at his
funeral, by Robert L. Fulton:

"One of the founders of our community lies dead today.   Charles T. Bender was at the city's beginning
and no one was more loyal to Reno when he died.   No
one contributed more to the up-building of Nevada's
material interests or to the development of her state-
hood. Making no pretense as a leader, his judgment was
sound and his advice was always good. His business as
a banker did not always conform with the demands of
philanthropy, but hundreds of men who today are successful men can trace the foundation of their fortunes
directly to his support and advice. "

Indeed the boys Father had trained in his bank had
gone out over the state to take jobs in other banks and

similar institutions.   They came back to Father with
their many problems and were always helped with wis-
dom and kindness.   At one time he counted thirty-four
that he had sent out into good jobs.   Senator Nixon of
Nevada, Frank Bell and Bob Moore, were some of the
names I can remember.

My Mother, Julia Bender, lived for many years after the passing her husband and some of the time was
spent at the home of my husband and I in Berkeley.
She still loved society affairs and one time really over-
did it! She belonged to a club in Los Angeles and spent
the winters there.   One time she expected to be given
a big party to welcome her to our home, and wanted me
to welcome all her club friends as I was the only daughter having a large enough home.   So she made out the
list for about sixty ladies to ask, but, before she got
through, she had doubled the number! I had to give the
party over a two day period!   It was fancy indeed, as
my mother always came to our home with new ideas in
the way of refreshments and this time she had me prepare individual oyster loaves, while the dessert was
made up of skinned long-finger grapes soaked in orange
juice.   The guests kept exclaiming over the delicious
repast so much that I almost forgave Mother for her
big party! The second day of the party the grapes took
so long to fix some of the guests of the first day's party
came in to help me get ready.

Mother was so delighted with her grand party she
started hinting she knew of lots of others to ask for a
third day! But I was too tired by that time and couldn't
get the help.   However, Mother never gave up having
parties whenever she could as long as she stayed with
us.

GIRLHOOD AND GIRLHOOD FRIENDS

I was born on July 15th of 1878 in Reno, Nevada, and my older sister, Clara, was born on July 18th, 1877. So we were two of the first children born in the newly-named town of Reno. That year my father was the chief telegrapher in Reno for the Central Pacific Railroad (now called the Southern Pacific), having opened that office through the efforts of his Uncle Edwin B. Crocker of Sacramento. Mr. Charles Crocker, one of the big four financiers of the Central Pacific, and brother of Judge Edwin Crocker, named the town after General Jesse Reno.

Mr. Lake, who owned the bridge over the Truckee and the small hotel near it, was a close friend of my Father's. His ranch was about 10 miles south of Reno, and the biggest fun of our very young lives was to go on picnics down to the Lake Ranch. What fun we would have jumping in the hay, racing through the fields and wading in the irrigation ditches.

When I was about six or seven years old, Aunt Margaret Crocker (my father's aunt) asked me to spend the summer at their Van Ness Avenue home in San Francisco to be a playmate for her granddaughter, Gladys. That great mansion, with all its appurtenances of wealth, was quite an experience for me, and I am suprised that I can't remember more about it, such as where I slept and where we had our meals. But I do remember our rides with a coachman and a nurse out to the beach where Gladys and I took off our shoes and stockings and ran out into the waves, or dug in the sand, making, with many a giggle and squeal of pleasure, our castles and tunnels and canals.

Before I came home, Aunt Margaret took me to

Bertha Bender
Age about 25

Bertha and Clara Bender
Ages 2 and 4

Edwin Bender in curls
of a 3 year old

Kate Bender
Age about 17

Florence Bender Carpenter
Age about 22

Jay Carpenter
Age about 24

Elizabeth and Clayton
Carpenter, 7 and 3

Clara Bender

Schonwasser's and bought me a lovely dress.   When I
told Mother that Aunt Margaret had paid $25.00 for it,
she took the wind out of my sails by saying:

"I could have gotten it for $10.00 . They always
charge Aunt Margaret a lot more!"

One time Aunt Margaret sent us a box of very gaudy
jewelry, the first on the market of the "costume jewelry" craze. Mother had been told that it was all made up
of fake stones, so she calmly sent it back to Aunt Margaret, telling her she had been cheated.   I guess that
ended our being in Aunt Margaret's good graces because
the children of Charles Bender were forgotten there-
after whenever Aunt Margaret invited children of other
relatives to go on trips.   But Mother continued to visit
the Crocker home on Van Ness Avenue after the Crock-
ers had moved there from Sacramento.

From such San Francisco visits Mother brought
back many exciting stories about Aunt Margaret's
youngest daughter, Annie, who was making a dashing
and expensive display of herself in San Francisco society. Mother told often of her terrible extravagances,
made often just to startle people.   She always drove to
town in grand style and wouldn't wear rain coats when
it rained, but would simply go into a store and buy a
whole new outfit.   She finally married Porter Ash and
had one child by him, Gladys, my playmate, who was
later kidnapped by him, after a divorce, and was, I suppose, paid for with high stakes.

Jenny Crocker, the older sister, married my
mother's cousin, Sloat Fassett of Elmira,   New York,
and was a very different person and beloved by all the
family relatives.   She often came to San Francisco and
always gathered relatives on both sides to luncheons,
usually held at Taits on the Beach.

At times our family would be sent one pound boxes of caramel candies from friends in San Francisco, but these delights would disappear so fast that it always seemed to me that one piece would scarcely have time to melt in my mouth before our big family would dispose of the rest! But one time I happened to be in San Francisco, waiting for a train to take me home to Reno, and had the extraordinary fortune of having $5.00 in my pocket, given to me as a birthday present. Never did money so want to burn a hole in a pocket! I was near a Maskey's Candy Shop and immediately rushed over there and ordered a five pound box of their best caramels before my more sober conscience could get the better of me. I decided this would be a present for the whole family, but, just to make sure I got all I wanted myself, I ordered an extra pound to eat on the train.

Well, I had to wait and wait for that big box. I would go up and ask about it and they would always say that yes, they were getting it ready, but it seemed to me it took hours. Finally I got my box onto the train and then stayed up most of the night eating my pound of candy and developing a bad conscience while doing it, as I imagined Father and Mother saying how foolish I was to spend all that money on candy! When I arrived at Reno I was so full of candy that I didn't care about any more for a month, and so full of remorse that I flung myself into Father's arms, weeping bitterly, and crying:

"I got a candy box for the whole family, but now I wish I hadn't!"

Father comforted me, however, by saying:

"It isn't every little girl who would spend all her own birthday money buying candy for her family. I think it was a very nice thing to do!"

Throughout my childhood my oldest sister, Clara

was the big protector for all of us and also our boss.
She was unusually strong and of a very dominant character. When she got a certain look in her eyes nobody dared to cross her except Father. She was not
afraid at all of even the biggest boys of the neighbor-
hood. I remember Homer, the oldest of my two brothers, hollering when a bigger boy was beating him up.
Clara came running up, grabbed that boy by the seat of
his pants, boxed his ears with a sound you could hear
for a block, and tossed him through the air about six
feet onto his nose. He never bothered Homer again!
As for Edwin, our littlest brother, no boy dared even
look cross-eyed at him when Clara was around!

Clara lost the sight of both eyes, but was cured by
the famous Dr. Barcans of San Francisco. She was a
wonderful designer of clothing and kept us all in the lat-
est styles. Later she married Frank Humphrey, a Nevada rancher, who idolized her. She had two sons,
Marvin and Frank Ellis, but unfortunately died before
the youngest was two years old. I took care of those
two handsome boys for over a year. Marvin has since
become a Nevada legislator and a fine businessman in
Reno. Ellis is a businessman in California.

Clara and I considered our two younger sisters, Kate
and Florence, somewhat on the spoiled side, which I
guess was natural for older sisters to think. Kate was
very finicky about the food she ate and Florence was
equally finicky about her clothing. Kate got the finest
education of any of us at the University of Nevada and
was a teacher for awhile. She later married George
Ross Worn, a lumberman of note and member of a fine
early California family. They had one son, Charles,
now a surveyor of California highways.

Florence was the beauty of the family, but she added to the beauty a very loving and gentle disposition,

which made it difficult for her less favored sisters to be very jealous of her.   She was Mother's favorite, and Mother, Clara and I often worked hard to put Florence into pretty clothes.   She married Jay A. Carpenter, who had graduated magna cum laude from the University of Nevada.   As a young mining engineer, he took her as a bride into many rough mining camps, but latter gave her a more settled life when he became, first, a professor of mining at the University of Nevada, and, later, Director of the institution's famous Mackay School of Mines.   They had two wonderful children, Elizabeth, now the wife of a mining engineer herself, O. Perry Riker of Reno, and Clayton, an electrical engineer with the physical plant department at the University of Nevada.

For myself, I could claim three qualities not possessed in such degree by my sisters.   One was an ability to sew fine stitches and do attractive knitting. Another was an ability to get up early in the morning to get my work done.   And the third was a knack for baking fine cakes, cookies, candies and doughnuts. This latter ability, however, was put to good use by my sisters during our courting days.   Many a time Florence or Clara or Kate would trot out my cookies or cakes or doughnuts before the young men who came to visit them, bemusing them with the natural inference that they had cooked them!   I went along with this mild deceit, hoping my sisters would not later disillusion the three young men who became their husbands!

Probably the most annoying cross I had to bear during my childhood was my name, Bertha, which I loathed exceedingly, spending many hours dreaming of how fine it would be to be called Pearl!   I even tried to insist that this was my name at one time, but was laughed out of it by the rest of my family.   However, what was even more difficult to bear was that I alone among all in the family had not been given a middle name. Such are the woes of childhood forced on helpless infants by unknowing parents! It was rather comical that later my husband and I foisted on our son the first name of "Duart," which he exceedingly disliked for the very good reason that other boys started calling him "Warty." However, we had given him an escape with the middle name of "Vinson, " which he thankfully appropriated as his only usable fore-name, dropping the first.

Homer, though younger than I, was the steady older brother in our family, and certainly the hardest worker of the two. Father sent him down river to the Trosi Ranch to learn milking, and this lesson Edwin contrived not to learn, so Homer was always the milker. But Edwin did love that rich milk! Homer was most interested in technical things. So he was naturally the one to help Father rig up the telegraph line to the bank. An extension of this line to a boy friend's house, however, was very nearly Homer's undoing, as he fell out of a cottonwood tree, where he was fixing the line, and down about twenty feet! A picket fence fortunately, but painfully, broke his fall!

I came to feel later that Father allowed Homer to work too hard, especially when working with too heavy loads as a teen-ager injured his back. Homer showed unusual courage by earning his own money to go back to Boston Tech (now Massachusetts Institute of Technology) and get an engineering degree, all over the objections of Father. He married Susan Bower, the daughter of an early doctor in West Virginia, a small and quiet person, but whom we found made an extraordinarily neat house wife and a fine and gentle mother. Homer has been a successful civil and electrical engineer, now retired in Spokane, Washington. Their oldest son, David, distinguished himself as a brilliant, straight A student at

California Institute of Technology and went on to build a fine career as a physicist in important government and university work. His younger brother, Philip, has a stable and happy family life as an electrical technician in Clarkson, Washington.

Edwin, my youngest brother, was an unusually adventurous boy and was constantly getting into scrapes. I remember a time when we had dinner at our friends, the Lyman's house, and Edwin, about four at the time, showed off and acted so outrageously that Father had to send him home in disgrace.

Perhaps the most scary happening with Edwin was when he fell into the big flume of rushing water above Verdi about ten miles west of Reno, it all happening when we were on a picnic. In our desperation to get down below and catch him, Father started us all in the wagon down the grade only to discover that one of the horses would not hold back on the steep road and that our wonderful horse, Granger, could not do it alone. So down the turns we rushed at break-neck speed, with Father standing up and wildly pulling at the reins while praying that we would make it below. Edwin was successfully rescued, but Father nursed sore arms for a week because of that experience.

Aunt Margaret Crocker probably added to Edwin's semi-delinquency by sending him a Shetland pony to ride. It wasn't long before Edwin was scandalizing the staid people of Reno by riding the pony at breakneck speed down Virginia Street pretending he was a cowboy! Father had to tell him that such places were off limits, but Edwin continued his wild ways with the shetland when he could. This pony was on the vicious side, and, when I rode him once, he knew I was afraid of him and brushed me close along a picket fence. I was black and blue for weeks and never rode him again.

He finally chased Homer, the oldest brother, and knocked him down and would have pawed him to death if the hired man hadn't been close at hand and rushed up to save him. After that, as can be imagined, Father soon got rid of our Shetland pony!

Edwin enlisted in the Naval Air Force during the First World War and took his training at Camp Pensecola, Florida, but didn't get into action. Certainly cruising the freedom of the blue skies suited his nature. While in the Navy, but after the war, he married Adele Norcross, the daughter of Judge Frank Norcross of Carson City. They had one son, Frank Norcross Bender, who is now running the family business, the Bender Warehouse Company in Reno. Edwin, with the help of this son, and his nephew, Charles Worn, had established this business in 1946, after earlier business experiences in banking and a restaurant. Edwin died, of unknown back complications, in 1952. His widow now runs a very successful business, The Wedding Shop, in Reno.

Once I appeared in Piper's Opera House in Reno with a number of school girls as a part of a school show. We were dressed to represent the styles and costumes of different years. I was with a group of four wearing bloomers of the future. When we stepped onto the stage we were thoroughly hooted and hissed at by a group of boys in one of the side boxes until our conversation was drowned out completely. I had written my speech on the back of a fan in case I forgot. But everybody forgot their parts and we didn't appreciate our reception!

One of the things that really delighted us in the early days was to ride in a one-horse sled behind Granger, our wonderful horse, with the bells tinkling, the whip cracking and the snow tossing up on all sides. But one time the most embarrassing incident of my life happened when I was riding in the sled behind Granger and Father was cracking the whip. For some reason Granger shied at something he saw in the snow and whipped the sled around in such a way that I was tossed out head-first into the snow bank. It was right by the railroad track where a section gang was at work clearing away snow, and several of the men rushed over and dragged me out of the snowbank feet first and upside down. I blushed all the way home and stayed away from the railroad tracks for some time!

Two young men who kept us in stitches of laughter when we were children were my Uncle Charley and his good friend, Joe Dillman. They were both in many amateur shows, and once Joe was invited to be the orator in a Fourth of July program. As he was quite a Beau Brummell and often called on the girls at the Whittaker Seminary in Reno, his friends joked a lot about his coming speech, and one said:

"Joe, you must be very careful when you announce at the end of your speech that 'we will now proceed to the cemetery,' not to say 'seminary' instead!"

When the time came for the speech "seminary" was the exact word Joe used, much to the shock of the more staid people of Reno!

One of my chums in Reno, Ivy Evans, married much younger than I did, but her marriage to one of the Sharon family of Oakland was very unhappy and led soon to divorce. I attended court with her in Virginia City, Nevada, to lend any assistance I could.

Her mother was very fond of me and we three had happy visits together. The mother had come from the East with two children and had married one of three brothers by the name of Evans and bore him two children. Alvero Evans later became an alcoholic and lost his fortune.

Three sisters in mid-life,
Kate, Bertha, Florence

Bertha Bender Brown
and son, Vinson

Edwin Bender as Naval
Air Lieutenant, 1918

Three cousins, Elizabeth,
Clayton and Vinson

Elizabeth Carpenter
Age about 18

Charles Worn as Army
Captain, with Frank
Bender (ensign in wa

Susan Bowers Bender
and David, 1 year old

Homer Bender
Age about 20

Alvero had one of the same breed of horses as my father's wonderful Granger. The horse would take the old man to town each day and then, if he became hungry or it looked stormy, he would not wait for the old fellow to come out of the saloon, but would go by himself to the Hymers Livery Stable and walk into the stall that was always held for him for the day. Promptly at 5 P. M., so prompt that people set their watches by him, the horse would arrive at the saloon to pick up the old man. Sometimes Alvero was unable to hold the reins, a minor matter to the wise old horse, who would calmly walk home, always pausing at the railroad track to look each direction and make sure no train was coming!

The Evans family owned a large section of the northwest part of Reno, but they became poor with property and finally had to go into the chicken business. Ivy, my friend, was as dainty a person as I ever knew, but she pitched in on all the hard work of the chicken ranch and managed to make a living for herself and mother. Her mother was a very wise old person and could interest me by the hour with her good horse sense. One time she told me that whenever things became bad and worrysome for her, she just sat herself down and calmed herself by saying, "The Lord will provide."

She told how one day she and Ivy went into their separate rooms for a rest and nap. When they awakened this day, they found nothing to eat in the house, so Ivy wanted to go to the nearest grocery to get cookies, but both were so tired from their work that Mrs. Evans told Ivy not to go and just sat down, folded her hands and said quietly, "the Lord will provide."

Unknown to both ladies the Lord indeed provided! Mrs. Evans son, Pug, who was quite a fisherman, had come into the house with a friend while the women slept. He was taking this friend, a prominent Reno lawyer, on a special fishing trip, but the lawyer was carrying a cake he was supposed to deliver to his wife for a tea she was giving.

"Leave it on the dining room table," said Pug, "and we will pick it up when we come back with our fish."

What was the surprise of the two ladies to discover this fine cake on the table! Soon they were gratefully eating it, and shared some with another son who came home about this time. With second helpings, the cake was soon all gone, and they were congratulating themselves on the wonderful way the Lord had provided for them, when Pug and the lawyer came home. One can imagine the lawyer's outraged cry when he found his wife's tea party cake completely vanished!

One family who lived near us included a lady who was quite a fancy dresser and constant talker. They kept a cow and it was often quite startling to see the wife milk that cow either in the morning or evening as she would invariably be dressed in a garishly colored red, pink, green or other bright colored evening gown, although an old one of course.

Another neighbor included a wife who was a real loud talker and she hated to see her two daughters have much fun. One morning the circus was in town and the tents were down by the railroad tracks, one block from our home. We kids were all waiting to fly to the corner to see the parade, as it started from the center of town, and, when we heard the drums and instruments start up, we all beat it for the corner to watch. But our neighbor's daughter suddenly heard her mother shout:

"Where are you going?"

"I'm going to see the elephants!"

"Well," yelled the mother, "you come right back here and see the elephant in my dish pan!"

Poor girl, I can still remember the utterly stricken look on her face. And so it was always with her, she could never have a bit of fun!

One year the famous heavyweight championship fight between Bob Fitzsimmons and Jim Corbett was held in Nevada and, for some days, both fighters and their trainers were working-out on the outskirts of Reno. It happened one day that a girl friend and I were seated on top of a tall stone gate post down by the river when the two parties met by accident. Somehow two dogs, one from each camp, started fighting, and this triggered the whole meeting into a regular Donnybrook, with fighters, trainers and dogs trading blows and bites all over the place! The neighbors soon called the police to stop it, but meanwhile we two girls were delighted and frightened both to have a preview of the big fight, something proper young ladies in those days were not even supposed to think about!

I went to the University of Nevada for only one year, but during that year I rose to be a Captain in the Girl Cadet Corps. I don't understand to this day why they chose me because I certainly didn't make much of a success out of disciplining the four to eight girls I had under me. There was one irrepressible young lady whose every action was funny. Though I would give a stern command, she had a perfectly astounding knack of turning it into a shout of glee. We were often asked to step out of the line until we could control our almost uncontrollable laughter! Her name was Maude Haines and some of her children still live in Reno. She became one of my dearest friends.

In the Mackay School of Mines at the University appeared some brilliant young men, and many went to far places and became famous mining engineers. It was the crowning glory of my life to come out ahead of those boys in one class, geometry! I remember so well taking one examination at the end of the term. It was so easy for me that I got through in in half the time, and left the room, the object of many envious stares. Many thought, however, that I couldn't solve the problems and was giving up. What was their utter astonishment to learn that I had received 100% in the final exam! But algebra was another story and, in that class, I was as poor a fish as anybody else.

Dr. Joseph E. Stubbs was President of the University when I was attending and I was in his class in German, which I enjoyed very much as he was as perfect a teacher as you could wish for. But I fell asleep more than once in his class, due to not feeling well, and was so grateful that he had the sensitivity to understand my condition and would gently dismiss me from class until I felt better. He was truly a gentleman! In my loyalty and gratitude I would return and hand in more than the work required.

Perhaps no sound in early Reno days comes back so much to my mind and heart as the sound of the trains, the old-fashioned steam trains, now all gone. Being only a block from the tracks, we would hear, every night, the deep roaring and chugging of the giant engines as they gathered their flocks of box cars to pull up over the steep grades to Truckee and beyond over the Donner Summit in the high Sierras. The clicking of the wheels on the rails, the shudder and crash as two sections were locked together, the long-drawn whistles, so much sharper on cold nights, and then the solid roaring as the engines gathered head and steam for the long steep haul, these are the remembered music of my girlhood.

I look back on all those early days as through a rosy glow. Reno was truly a wonderful and exciting town in which to grow up!

SERVANTS OF THE FAMILY

In the early days in Reno we had many kinds of help for our large family, as wages were low and labor-saving appliances non-existant. We almost always had Paiute or Washoe Indian squaws come to do our cleaning, washing and ironing.

One very fine one, a Paiute of large size and friendly disposition, was Allie, and she was with us many years. She seemed to have several different husbands, changing them almost by the year, and numerous children, who usually appeared with her and stayed out in our large back yard. Sometimes the man would cut wood, but all of them were always ready for a lunch, which usually included a big pot of tea, bread and whatever was left from our table. Sometimes we made up stew, which they liked with plenty of gravy.

One husband seemed to have the regular habit of beating up Allie, and she would stay home long enough to recover, then show up again at our house. Another husband took a shot at her and then killed himself. Luckily for her, she dropped so suddenly when he fired at her that he thought she was dead. But she mourned for him a long time, plastering her face with mud.

After this another swarthy brown husband appeared who called my father "Charley" and my mother "blue old woman." When she asked him to do anything, he would reply, "Me wait for Charley when he come home!" He wanted no woman to boss him!

Once my oldest sister, Clara, went down to see Allie and take her some food. She found her small cabin very homelike because it was overflowing with things we and our neighbors had given her at one time or another.

One day, after we were all grown up, my sister Kate called up Florence to say Allie was on her usual yearly visit. She always came expecting a handout in either clothes or money. At this time she was living in Winnemucca - about 170 miles from Reno - and so she had come quite a ways. When Florence appeared, Kate said:

"Allie, do you remember Florence?"

"Oh yes," said Allie, "she wear too many panties!" I expect that Allie didn't appreciate Florence wanting a clean pair every day, as, with four girls in the house, that was too much ironing and Allie saw no use for that!

The Indians, I am sure, were just as critical of our foibles and weaknesses as we were of theirs, turn about being fair play. One day we were all down at the depot to meet some friend, but a freight train came through first. It screeched to a stop and one brakeman was thrown between the cars in such a way that his leg was badly crushed. There was much excitement and talk about this and I became faint at the sight. I felt myself going under unless I could reach something to hold onto. I walked to a large post and missed my grab for it, falling to the ground in a dead faint!

Unfortunately for me, a circle of Indian Squaws were playing cards close by and saw my performance, which they thought was a great joke and roared and rocked with laughter about it. They had probably come to the depot, hoping for some money to be thrown to them by passengers on the train, but this humiliation of a young white lady was better than any money! For a long time after this I dreaded seeing Indians approaching me on the street, for, if one were a squaw, she would invariably stop and stare, then begin to giggle loudly and point at me, informing the others about me until all would laugh.

We had few nurses in Reno in those days, but one, Mrs. Barker, came all the way from San Francisco to help us when the younger ones in the family were born. Homer, the oldest of my two brothers, was helped into the world by her, and so she was present when the carollers, led by Dick Jose, who later became a famous concert singer, were singing outside at the time of his birth, "Hail the New Born King" on Christmas Eve. And soon she was coming up twice a year to help us out.

Abby, as we called her, was a striking looking woman of very strong character, and had a colorful history, as she had come around the Horn as a stowaway on an early steamer. She claimed she was escaping from a husband that she could not bear any longer to live with.

Abby's first job every spring was to give us all a good and generous dose of sulphur and molasses. My sister Clara despised this stuff worse than any of us, and, being an unusually strong girl, put up a terrific fight every time Abby came, running away from her and screaming until our Dad put his foot down and said it had to be taken.

Abby Barker lived in that place of romance, "The City" (San Francisco), and besides this had incredible adventures as a nurse out to many of the old mining camps in California and Nevada where she was often called. She made quite a favorite out of me, doing so many kind things, that it later became a sentimental pilgrimage to visit her at the Crocker Old People's Home in San Francisco where my mother had helped get her a room.

Always, when I went to the "City," I would go to see her, and always found her waiting for me at the head of the stairway. She knew when I would come, though I had not sent her word.

We also had a jolly Irish girl come twice a year to make up clothes for the family. While mother could sew well enough and made beautiful button holes, she could not give all her time to it. We had a large sewing room built onto the kitchen and one door from this led into the dining room. Anna had blazing red hair, and came from Virginia City. She finally married a man in Truckee, California and we missed her a lot. To get along without her we had a hand sewing machine revised into an electric machine on which we could do all the ruffles, tucks and so forth. It was many years later that the real electric machines came on sale.

One time, I remember, we three older girls were asked to help one lady who gave many parties as there were no cateresses then. So we became very popular, along with a few other young ladies, to wait on table not only at this home but others. We had to look our best for these parties and often came home all aglow because of the compliments received for our attractively made clothes, often designed by our talented sister, Clara.

One day we all felt abused because we thought we needed new coats, but we didn't get any sympathy from our mother. We had to dress up that afternoon to serve as cateresses at a party given by a lady across the river, and, in passing by the bank in town, decided to go in and make Father feel ashamed that we didn't have new coats. He looked up from his papers and, with a broad smile at seeing us, said:

"Why, how nice you do all look! When did you get those nice new coats? You were kind to stop in to show them to me!" We left rather downfaced, but later concluded he had been warned of our purpose and was really teasing us!

Many old Reno families used to have Chinese cooks, but we never tried one. We did have, however, for many years, a most wonderful Japanese cook named Uchida. He was not only a fine cook, but a most extraordinary character. He had recently come from Japan

Marvin Humphrey
Age about 6

Frank Ellis Humphrey
Age about 4

David Bender
Age about 6

Philip Bender
Age about 4

Uchida and family in Japan, about 1955

Group of Paiute Indians
   near SP Station, Reno
(Photo Calif. Hist. Soc.)

Mrs. Abby Barker,
Nurse to the famil

and could, at first, speak little English, but once my mother found out his sterling qualities, she hung on to him for dear life. I cannot express too much how we all loved and respected Uchida, so that these funny stories about him show only the natural humor of how a a young man from a country strange to us found it hard to adjust himself to America. No doubt if one of us had gone to Japan under similar conditions, many of our actions would appear equally funny to the Japanese!

Some of the rich divorcees who came to Reno soon heard about his marvelous cooking and tried many times to lure him away from us. They would call him up on the telephone and the conversation would sound like this:

"Yes, this Uchida." -- "Yes, but I am not wanting another place." -- "Yes, but I do not want more money." -- "Yes, but I am very happy here." ---- "But, please, this is my home! Goodbye!"

He certainly loved our family very much and over the years again and again proved his loyalty. But there were two things that made Uchida very unhappy. One was when he was told by Mother that his kitchen had to be cleaned up, washed and painted. He always left at such a time, using a plausible excuse, such as a sick cousin, or some urgent business. And he was always most apologetic and "so sorry," but also quite firm.

In about a month the phone would ring and it would be Uchida, wanting to speak to Mrs. Bender. He would always say: "Mrs. Bender; I come home now!" An event and remark that would happen every year.

Another thing that made him "so very sorry" was when wild ducks were bought or given to us. That was just too much, he thought, and would look so very sad until all the family pitched in to help pick and clean them. Then he would cook them as nobody else ever could, or so we all thought.

Once Father was persuaded to purchase a gun and go on a hunting trip, which he had never done before. He told Mother to ask people for dinner, as he surely counted on bringing home some ducks. Well, he and his friend, who guided him, did get a duck, but they were two very disappointed hunters. But mother assured them she would have a good dinner anyway. It just happened that the town hunter and fisherman came to the back door that very morning "with ducks aplenty," as Uchida said, and the whole family, except Father, who was at the bank, got busy.

Later, at the table, when Uchida brought in our largest platter with ducks and ducks, dripping over the sides, Father's eyes nearly popped with surprise.

"Now, where in the world did you get these?" he asked, and Mother replied:

"Well, I just went hunting!"

Uchida was so happy that he danced around the table, and then smiled and bowed at every compliment about his fine cooking. He loved to do the honors and serve at the table whenever there was company, as he was sure to be able to bask in the glow of many remarks about the excellence of the food. "So happy!" he would say, with his kindly face wreathed in smiles, "yes, so happy!"

As the years passed Uchida was present to do the honors and be "so happy" at each of our weddings.

When Father bought his first car, it was big enough to take all the family and Uchida decided he wanted to be the family chauffeur. He was taught by a friend and got along fairly well after awhile, but we will always remember his first trip to get father at the bank at noontime. Uchida forgot how to stop the car, so he just drove it right into the double bank doors, which were placed across the corner of the building. "Oh, so sorry Mr. Bender!" was repeated over and over all the way home.

Another time he agreed to drive the second maid around the block. She was a French or Spanish Basque, and a very wild looking person and most excitable. Uchida made her sit on the back seat, but he went around the first corner so fast that Felicia grabbed him around his neck and hung on! He couldn't get her to let go and, in the excitement, forgot how to stop the car. Careening round and round the block, he began to shout "Mama, Mama! Help, oh help!" Finally the man who had taught him got onto the running board and managed to stop them. Uchida was very red in the face, and also, "so sorry!"

At a still different time Uchida came running up from the cellar after the furnace had back-fired, shouting: "Mama! Mama! House afire!"

Mother had to be equal to all emergencies, so she stopped the smoking of the furnace and calmed Uchida down all at the same time!

My husband, Dr. Henry A. Brown, and I lived two blocks from my old home, while Florence and her husband, mining engineer, Jay Carpenter, lived across the street. Uchida made such wonderful dinner rolls that we hated to miss them, so, after he served the first course at home, he would get on his bycycle, come down the two blocks to my house with piping hot rolls, then back to Florence's house with rolls for her. In the meantime Father would be impatient, wondering whether he was going to get his dinner at all. But he never found out about Uchida's trips to share those wonderful rolls with us!

Uchida finally decided he didn't want to be a cook any more, as we were all married off. So Father helped him get started in the insurance business, which was fine until he couldn't find anymore Japanese in the state of Nevada to insure! So then he went into business and opened the first fish store in Reno, with which he flourished for some years.

But Uchida was never too busy to bake an apple pie for me when I went home to visit, and he would often call me up and say: "Miss Bertha, I take you calling. I have a car. I be your chauffeur!"

Uchida made quite a study of horse racing, and, often, when the race track opened for its week or two stay in Reno, Uchida left the fish market to make money out of the racing. At the track he was always "so happy" to see us. We were told that he did very well on the races.

Finally Uchida went back to Japan with his family of "five too many," as he told me on one of his yearly visits to Reno. Now he is in Japan and we have his family picture of three boys and one girl, all grown, and all wanting to get back to America.

STORIES OF UNCLE HENRY YERINGTON

When Henry Marvin Yerington, the grand old man of Carson City and the Manager of the Virginia and Truckee Railroad, married the youngest sister of my father, Clara, there was a great buzzing of tongues in Nevada, as she was more than twenty years younger than he. But rarely was there a happier marriage, since all the dignity and powerful masculinity of the man was offset by a gentleness, courtesy and love that was repaid with deep affection by the radiant and beautiful girl.

His personality and character had a deep effect on my family, and, to my notion, he was as colorful a human being as ever lived in Nevada. When Edwin C. Hill was giving his interesting talks on the radio many years ago, he gave a most fascinating lecture on Uncle Henry that was repeated several times. He said that people in the East always had the idea that there was no culture or refinement out west, especially in Nevada. Then he pictured the man he considered the most interesting character in Nevada, H. M. Yerington, Superintendent of the Virginia and Truckee Railroad. He described his wonderful white hair, beautiful suits, the elegant ties he wore, and even the red carnation in his buttonhole that was supplied by a San Francisco florist the year around. And he went on to describe his many kindnesses and courtesies to others, his clock-like running of the V. and T. Railroad, and his tremendous dignity and piercing eyes.

Uncle Henry had a great dislike for Reno, I suppose because the main railway line went through to the East that way instead of through his beloved Carson City. He did concede, however, that there were probably at least two honest men in Reno, one being my Dad, Charley Bender. But this respect and liking was strained to the limit one day when he came to see Dad at the bank. Like most leading railroad men of his time, Uncle Henry often tried to exert considerable political pressure on others. So this day he attempted to tell our Dad how to vote. Dad looked him straight in the eye and told him where he could go and that he, Charles Bender, was going to vote as he pleased!

Uncle Henry stalked out of the bank like a great white-topped storm cloud, and, when Dad came home that night, he told Mother:

"Well, there won't be any more passes over the V. and T. I insulted H. M. today!"

But, when Christmas came, there appeared as gifts the usual letter with passes enclosed from Uncle Henry, with a note saying, "let the children come over for a visit!"

Uncle Henry was born in London, Canada, or very near there. When quite young he became the private secretary to an official of the Canadian Government. When on the way to a government meeting with some officials in a distant city, the train he was travelling on ran off the tracks, going over a trestle into a river. Uncle Henry was the only one alive who was pulled out of the river and the shock of the experience was so terrible that his hair turned white.

He later went into railroad work in Detroit and finally landed in Carson to help in building the V. and T. Railroad. Tall and dignified, he attracted attention everywhere, particularly because of his beautiful white hair, which was as fine as silk and very distinguished in appearance. But, when he married the second time to a girl just the age of his oldest son, he felt he should dye his hair black to be more youthful looking. However, Aunt Clara never liked to see him use the dye and was sure that it would one day affect the brain. But she could never persuade Uncle Henry to change.

Uncle Henry had his hair dyed by a special French barber every time he went to San Francisco on business. On his way to San Francisco, he and Aunt Clara would come in a private railway car to Reno and wait in it at the depot for one of the main line trains to come along and pick their car up. Here, in the car, they would visit our family, as Uncle Henry hated to take even one step in Reno, and never, to my knowledge, visited our home there.

Through the years I am sure that Aunt Clara schemed as to how she could get rid of her enemy, the black dye. There finally came a time when Uncle Henry could not go to San Francisco because of the press of business at home, so he sent a letter to the barber telling him to mail the dye up to Carson City. When Aunt Clara saw the package arrive in the mail, she saw her chance and quietly got rid of it.

As the days passed and the black hair began to streak a little with white, Uncle Henry started to fume and fuss, and finally sent a violently worded telegram to the barber, wanting to know "what in H--- has happened to my black dye!"

The barber fired back a snappy reply saying he had sent it on such and such a date and had the receipt too! Uncle Henry then telegraphed that he was a liar and received and equally hot and positive telegram in reply. Meanwhile Aunt Clara kept as quiet as a little mouse, but watched with satisfaction as the black hair slowly faded and began to change to brilliant white. At the same time Uncle Henry was so mad that he forgot all about ordering a new bottle of black dye. By a few adroit mentionings of how strikingly handsome he was on the part of Aunt Clara and the aid of similar tributes he had from others, he was led by stages to accept his white hair as an advantage rather than a handicap and Aunt Clara's little plan was fully vindicated!

So startling and striking indeed was that white hair, full and thick above his broad forehead, that it was said truthfully of Uncle Henry in later years that he could walk with great dignity across the middle of Market Street in San Francisco, the busiest street in the West, and simply stop all traffic while he passed by holding up his gold-headed cane in a threatening manner!

Uncle Henry had three sons and one daughter by his first marriage and all lived in Carson City, except the daughter, Avery, who lived part time in Detroit with her mother's relatives. The youngest son was the special man to represent the state of Nevada at all the fairs. He was a charming man and well built and dressed.

The only son of Uncle Henry and Aunt Clara had a very tragic end, as, during the terrible flu epidemics of 1918-9, he had six or seven attacks, until the sleeping sickness germs caught hold of him and ran his health down hill to his death. This was the great sorrow of Aunt Clara's final years, long after Uncle Henry was dead, and our family did what we could to alleviate it.

The Palace Hotel in San Francisco was where Uncle Henry and Aunt Clara would stay when down to "the City." It was said that when he walked into the great central hall, with his glowing white hair, his tall and thin, but very upright and dignified figure, and his gold-headed cane, he was such an imposing figure that all conversation would stop and everybody would turn to look at him.

Uncle Henry M. Yerington   Aunt Clara Yerington

Main Street of Carson City, about 1924
(Photo courtesy of California Historical Society)

Virginia and Truckee Railroad engine at Carson City,
about 1890 (Photo courtesy Calif. Hist. Society)

along the Truckee River Reno Nev.

Scene along the Truckee River in Reno in early days.
(Photo courtesy California Historical Society.)

Once, when he arrived at the Palace without notice, he sent Aunt Clara up in the elevator and went to the office to register. Well, they had to tell him his room was occupied. He let out a roar of rage that even Aunt Clara heard seven stories up. She ran to the railing around the hall and could see her husband with his cane waving, threatening everyone from the manager down! Somehow the room was cleared and he was finally satisfied.

At the V. and T. Railway Depot in Carson City, Uncle Henry would come down almost every day for his inspection before one of the trains left. Everything had to be spick-and-span, with the engine and cars shining like mirrors and every bit of brass polished so that not even a speck of dust could be found anywhere. If anything was not right, Uncle Henry let the person who was responsible know about it real quick and in loud tones. Yet he was beloved by most of his employees because of his many small kindnesses to their families.

Perhaps the chief tragedy in Uncle Henry's life was his loss of hearing. Uncle Henry was getting deaf in one ear, and, when he went to San Francisco to see a specialist, the ear was operated on. But, unfortunately, the doctor operated on both ears and Uncle Henry never heard a word again! It was a dreadful thing to have happened and that doctor should have been sued!

Life after this became very difficult for Uncle Henry, as, having to ask people to write their messages, and talking in a loud voice because he could not hear himself, made him sound much more gruff and quick-tempered than he really was.

But he never cowed Aunt Clara. Once when I was with them, he was upset because the cook hadn't done something right. After angrily telling Aunt Clara and her faithful maid what they should have done, he was astonished to see Aunt Clara write on her pad: "Any time you want to make a change here, you can go get someone else to run your home!"

He just meekly answered, "God Bless my soul!" as much as to say, "You are the only one who would dare say that to me!"

Aunt Clara told of his taking her abroad and, because of his deafness, what sad times she often had with him. They were guests one week end of Lady Heskible, who had been Florence Sharon of Palace Hotel fame, and had married an English nobleman. Their first breakfast was a buffet affair and they were supposed to help themselves. He did not like that and spoke up loudly to complain, though sure that he was only whispering to his wife. But everybody heard him!

By the time they got through this meal, she decided they had to leave. The host and hostess were not there and no one introduced them to the others. It was certainly not a good place for them to be, with his outspoken habit.

A more humorous story she told was about a wild ride she took one day when her husband told her she could go along on a trip he was making, taking some officials up to Virginia City. Some ladies, living in Gold Hill, next to Virginia City, had called upon her in Carson City when she was a bride and she hadn't been able to return the call. So she determined to return their favor on this trip and got dressed up beautifully to go.

At that time dresses were worn long and full and hats were very big, especially those for summer. So she had on her beautiful clothes and Uncle Henry telegraphed ahead for horses and carriage to take her calling in style. She made three calls and then one lady was not in, so, at the last place, she had a long time to wait before the train would be at the depot. She dismissed the carriage, but told the man to be sure to come back for her and he promised he would.

During the time of waiting one of the real Washoe zephyrs came up, and, if you have ever lived in Nevada, you will know what she was up against! The wind soon was whipping the branches of the trees into a frenzy, and, when the driver did not come back, her hostess became greatly concerned as there was no way to reach anybody in those days because of no telephones.

Finally the hostess saw her milkman coming in his high-seated wagon, and she asked him to take Aunt Clara to the depot. He was willing, but Aunt Clara could not reach the step to get up on the seat, so he just picked her up and put her there! Then he had to whip up his horses to make the depot on time.

As they dashed madly through the streets, with the wind blowing like a great stampede around them, and sending clouds of dust stinging through the air, Aunt Clara began to feel her beautiful feathers leaving her hat in clusters and every few moments her skirts would fly clear over her head! Her feet couldn't reach the dash board so she was just swaying back and forth as the horses plunged down hills and around the corners.

The driver had his hands full with the horses, but managed now and then to reach over to her knees and push her back on the seat, while she grabbed onto his arm and grabbed to save her beautiful hat. Then her long hair began to fall, so that she was certainly a sight as they came around the last corner with the horses plunging madly, the driver pulling her dresses down and then pushing her knees back! Then he pulled her to a stop so suddenly in front of the depot that it upset her completely. So, in desperation, he just picked her up bodily and threw her into her husband's outreached arms. And all Uncle Henry could say was, "God bless my soul!"

When she was through with her story, all my guests of the day were in gales of laughter, and, ever since, whenever I met any of them, they would bring back the memory of my charming aunt and her stories.

Aunt Clara's dressmakers lived in San Francisco and everything she wore was exquisite and of beautiful and expensive materials imported from France or England. She had a closet as big as most people's rooms. The piles of boxes in that room were very intriguing and I often wished I could be turned loose in there to see into them. The three dressmakers were sisters who had come to San Francisco from Paris, Rappetti, I believe by name.

As Aunt Clara and her foster-daughter, Avery, with most always my help, would be busy for weeks before Easter preparing for their special church fair, then was the time I had my wish to see this room fulfilled. The boxes would all be brought down and the materials within them made into beautiful bags, pin cushions, fancy boxes, and so forth. Both ladies were clever at developing attractive gifts, and, as I could do a great deal of the fine stitches, such as feather stitching and embroidery of many kinds, my time was well taken up.

Aunt Clara's dresses, as well as those of her friend, Mrs. Edmund Lyman, are still in the San Francisco Museum in Golden Gate Park. Mrs. Lyman was the wife of the Superintendent of one of the large mines and evidently dressed beautifully in the style of the day, as Aunt Clara did. Aunt Clara always wore white winter and summer clothes. I believe her house dresses were of the shirt waist type, but way ahead of that time, as we know them, and of her own innovation. One special shoe man came to San Francisco once each year, and she bought her shoes from him and oftentimes had them made to order.

The Yeringtons lived high in Carson City, with a big, cool cellar, to keep meat, vegetables, and so forth. Many foods were shipped by express from the big markets in San Francisco. Three Chinese worked for them and their beloved maid, Ida. But many poor people were helped by them also, which is shown by the fact that Uncle Henry's beautiful and stately grave marker in Carson City has had, down through the years, lots of different bunches of lovely flowers on Decoration Day. I am sure many people have fond memories of his kindness and generosity that shone through the gruffness or bluster of his outer ways.

As the years went by Uncle Henry became very dear to me and he became very interested in whatever I was doing. I was in his and Aunt Clara's home a great deal. Going through school was interrupted by illnesses and, when I would partially recover, I would be sent to Carson to spend many weeks with Aunt Clara and Uncle Henry. I never was afraid of him, as so many children were because of his gruffness.

After dinner he always sat down for a game of solitaire and I would sit on the arm of his chair, watching him. My arm usually was around his neck and he would explain every move he made with the cards. One time he was ready to give up and put out his hands to gather the cards together. But I happened to see a move and grabbed his hands away. He looked so surprised, saying, "Now what the devil?"

But I made the move and the whole thing came out correct. Well, I came up quite a bit in his estimation, as he looked at me so amazed, and said, "I see you have some real card sense!"

After that we would discuss the moves together, and Aunt Clara said how much he loved that attention and friendship from his niece. He also had deep feelings of affection for other children of our family and loved to have them come visit him and Aunt Clara.

If possible Aunt Clara would get up a game of whist for him with friends, and sometimes a queer old lady would come in her bed robe and slippers. She lived across the street and was an expert whist player. They said she was also a fiend for reading French novels. Her name was Annie Atcheson and she became quite a town character, but always welcome for a game after dinner. Once, when she disappointed them, I was roped in for the game. I had never played before and so it was with misgivings that I agreed. But things went along beautifully, as, when in doubt, I would talk with Avery or Aunt Clara about what I had and what I should play. Of course Uncle Henry couldn't hear what was going on, but, if he and I won the game, he would say:

"Well, I have met the first Bender with any card sense!" He made it a bit hard for me to live up to!

He had a wicker carriage to take his drives into the country with, and a beautiful horse called "Blackie." I wasn't too fond of riding with such a horse, and I had to keep a stiff upper lip when taken for a drive, as the carriage was imported from Germany and it seemed as if we were sitting so close to the back and powerful legs of that big horse that we could have been kicked to pieces very easily.

When I wrote to Uncle Henry and Aunt Clara that I was engaged to be married, he sent word over immediately that he wanted to see me. So I went to Carson and he began questioning me about my fiance, Dr. Henry Alexander Brown. I could tell him very little, knowing Alex for such a short time. I had to keep writing on the pad, "I don't know!"

Each time Uncle Henry would give a grunt of disgust. Finally, in despair, I wrote, "Well, he ought to be all right as he comes from your home town of London, Ontario."

Uncle Henry gave me a shake and said, "I don't care if he did; many a damn scamp came from there! You go back home and bring him over here and I will look him over myself!"

This finally happened and, fortunately, he was pleased, saying in such a loud whisper he could be heard for a block, "He's okay; I'll trust him!"

Uncle Henry finally became ill with some kidney trouble and doctors were brought from San Francisco to consult with the local physician. But he steadily became worse.

For a reason he would tell no one, he was very persistent in wanting to go to his office before he died, but all the doctors said, "No!" So he fired them all and said at last he could die in peace. Then he managed to send Aunt Clara on some kind of errand, and, when she was gone, he ordered his man nurse to get his clothes out and dress him and take him to his office. There he locked himself in and stayed for an hour alone. After that he came out, heaved a great sigh, and told the nurse he was ready to go home and die.

Aunt Clara was wild, not knowing what had happened to him. But, when he finally got into bed, he told her that he had had a lot of notes in the office that had been signed by poor people in the town to whom he had loaned money and that he had burned these all up as he wanted none of his family to try to collect money from those poor people. He also told her that there were thirty thousand dollars or more in the bank for her. With these things done and told, he was ready to meet his Maker, and he passed away the following day.

Aunt Clara sold her home in Carson City and moved to the Palace Hotel in San Francisco to be near her son, who was then in a hospital, fighting his terrible sickness. When Mr. Leonard, the Palace Hotel Manager, whom she liked, moved to take charge of the Fairmont Hotel on Nob Hill, she moved along with him. He was always very kind to her and, each anniversary of their move, her rooms were filled with beautiful red roses.

As her income dwindled at the last, she was taken care of at a cost she could afford. Also, another old friend and business associate of her husband, Ogden Mills (after whom is named the Mills Tower in San Francisco), let Mr. Leonard know that whenever she needed extra care, he would gladly come to her aid.

The last few months before she died, she spent the summer months with us out at our home at Castlewood Country Club near Pleasanton, California. While there she seemed to dwell on her early life in Carson. One day, especially, when I had ladies out from Berkeley for lunch, she entertained them with episodes of those early days, including those I have told here. It was wonderful to relive the life of that remarkable marriage and to hear so much of Uncle Henry again, but sad too. So do the years pass away and our memories only remain.

(Note: the town of Yerington, Nevada, was named after Henry M. Yerington.)

Bertha Bender Brown, about 1909

Dr. Henry Alexander Brown, about 1912

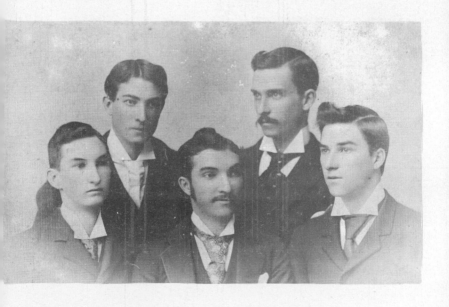

The five Brown brothers about 1888; John, Alex and Holmes in front row, Will and Arthur in back row.

Dr. and Mrs. Henry Alexander Brown with new Jordan

Dr. Brown as ship's surgeon,
about 1923

The Brown's home at 21
El Camino Real, Berkel

STORIES ABOUT DR. BROWN

My husband, Dr. Henry Alexander Brown, was born in London, Canada. His father was an editor of the London Free Press and also had a small farm near the town. He had four brothers, all of whom became professional men. The oldest was a Dentist and was the handsome one of the clan, named Authur. The others were Will, who became a lawyer in Los Angeles; Holmes, who was a newspaper editor in Spokane, Washington for years and knew well my beloved Uncle Charley; while the youngest was John, who became a famous ear, nose and throat specialist in Los Angeles. The father was of English descent from around Hull in Yorkshire, England, while the mother, Mary was of the McKenzie Scotch Clan of near Inverness, Scotland.

Alex, as I called him, left home quite early to make his own living, first moving to Chicago. He worked first for a dry goods house, being the janitor in the evening, clerk by day, and slept on the counter at night while acting as night watchman. Later he became a sales clerk for the famous Chicago department store of Marshall Field, in the men's clothing department and there learned what later became a fine taste and appreciation of well-made clothes. With the money earned, he financed his own way through medical school at the University of Pennsylvania, getting his M. D. degree somewhere around 1890. He continued his medical education later at London, Dresden and Berlin and polished it off with a final course in his eye specialty at the University of Prague soon after I married him.

When I met him first, he had just sold out a very fine practice in Nebraska and had bought the practice of an ear, nose and throat doctor in Reno, adding to this

his own eye work.   He was in on early pioneering in the fitting of glasses and uses of the first fine lenses to give sharp vision.   In those days it was often hard to sell people on their need for glasses, particularly as they considered the wearing of them a damage to their vanity, and it was sometimes both amusing and pathetic to see old people, who badly needed glasses, fumblingly try to find their mouths with food!   Women especially did not want to wear glasses as, to them, it was a definite sign of old age.

We went to Europe three times before the birth of our first and only child, Vinson, and Alex spent time in London, Germany and Prague to study under some famous specialists.   When Vinson was five we moved to Berkeley and Alex had offices there and in the City.

Our last trip to Europe was in 1928 when our son was fourteen years old, and we later regretted not taking him with us, as he could have learned a great deal.   But he was with his fine Aunt Florence and Uncle Jay Carpenter in Reno at the time, going to high school, and, for the first time, really learning how to study and also how to get along with his two cousins, Elizabeth and Clayton, who were near the same age.   So we hesitated to disturb his progress.   Later he had four trips on his own, between the ages of 17 and 24, to the Orient and Central America, where he got experience in observing and in writing about nature that was vital to his later career as an author and naturalist.

The funniest thing about this trip to Europe happened on the very first day.   Alex, as usual, was extremely busy and harried by a rush of patients to see him before he left, so I had to get everything ready myself.   He had been sighing and complaining for some days that he couldn't sleep because he was so nervous, but once he got to sea he knew he would completely relax and sleep like a child.   Meanwhile I had to handle him with kid gloves or he would blow up like a high pressure boiler!

I was ready to go early and went to his office to go to the boat with him, but his office girl wryly told me:

"Mrs. Brown, you get to that boat and pray! He has been worked to death and I have to handle him like a new baby!"

I did as she said and was soon at the boat waiting and waiting.   I had to go tell the German captain that my husband was late and I didn't know what to do. Finally, as the ladder of our German freighter was about to be drawn in, Dr. Brown came running and just made it! We went in to dinner and then right to bed.   He was asleep in two minutes while I lay awake for several hours.   Finally he awakened suddenly and said:

"Well, I feel like a different man already!"

I asked him where he thought we were.

"We must be outside the Golden Gate by this time," he replied.   He knew I was laughing and finally exclaimed in exasperation, "Well, where are we?"

"We are still at the wharf," I answered, "and have not moved an inch!"

Another funny thing that happened on that trip was the German crew trying to give us a royal Thanksgiving celebration. The spirit was good and their songs and other entertainment were wonderful, but we had a hard time hiding our disappointment when they brought out the turkey, all fine-sliced like a ham and far too dry! They meant well, but my how we missed the kind of juicy and well-basted turkeys we had at home!

Alex never learned to drive because of his very nervous disposition, but he did learn to back-seat drive and that with too much vigor for my taste. One time we were coming down Ashby Avenue in Berkeley and he became so obnoxious with his advice that I stopped the car, jumped out and ran around to his side, telling him to take over. He tried to do this, but, at Ashby and College Avenues he saw a car coming toward him down College and got so excited he pushed on the gas instead of on the brake! There was a sickening crash and then silence. Fortunately there was nobody hurt, but that was the last time he tried to drive, though by no means the end of his back-seat-driving!

One day in Los Altos he insisted I drive the wrong-way on a one-way street because he was so anxious to get to a meeting on time. A policeman stopped us and gave us a royal bawling out plus a ticket. After he had finished, I held up my hand and said:

"Officer, would you please tell my husband to let me do the driving after this!"

Alex opened his mouth to say something harsh, but then thought better of it and closed his lips. The policeman gave him a tongue lashing, and Alex controlled his back-seat-driving for about a month!

On the other hand, Alex had about the most tender heart towards animals and children that I ever saw in a man. During our years in Reno before we had our own child he was always bringing home after office hours some ragamuffin of a boy he had picked up, and would even talk yearningly about adopting them. One after another we would try them, but, though he was kind, he was too nervous to get along with them for long, and off each would go in time, sometimes with some of our money, silver or other valuables in their pockets! When our own baby arrived, I insisted that he stop trying to adopt others, but I am sure he always hankered for more in his heart.

For years he had two canaries that were the darlings of his life. Many minutes each day he would spend playing with Dicky, the father, and Peppy, the son. Peppy, in particular, loved to fight with Alex's finger and hop about on his shoulder scolding him ferociously! The two were almost inseparable and I never saw a man carry on so heart-brokenly as Alex did when Peppy suddenly caught sick and died. For days he hardly spoke a word and he swore that he would never again have another pet because he felt that he could not stand such a heartbreak. Something went out of his life when that merry little bird died, and he was never quite the same again.

Alex loved to tell stories about his adventures in different parts of the world and was not above adding a bit here and there to increase the drama. Not long before he passed away he spent part of a winter without me at the Hotel Vosburg at San Jacinto in southern California and there, I am sure, he had a field day with all the old ladies. Long afterward, when I was living down there myself, I would have many a lady come up to talk to me about "that fascinating husband of yours," and learn from their accounts that he had made some of the events in our lives that I had considered rather commonplace sound like the adventures of The Three Muskateers! However, I do not begrudge him his last fling at being "a man of the world."

My husband passed away at Los Altos in the fall of 1949 from a severe heart attack. I was so thankful that our son, Vinson, arrived home that evening to be with him in his last hours, and that Alex lived to see his son's first book published. He worried about his boy a great deal, but backed him always to the limit. Though their great difference in age caused too many misunderstandings, as did Alex's nervous ways, there was yet great love and respect between them.

SAN FRANCISCO TO
LOS ANGELES BY BIKE

In the 1890's bycycles were the new rage sweeping the country, especially among adventurous young people, and women in those days were making their first bid for freedom from domination by men. When the two events were combined into the story of the first two women to ride bycycles from San Francisco to Los Angeles, it was as big news as a new space adventure today. I remember almost dancing with excitement at the thought of being one of the women to go, though only seventeen.

Consider the tremendous difference in the state of the California roads in 1894 as compared to today. It was a dirt road most of the way, a twisting, rough dirt road at that, and lots of time no road at all! Often the crude road suddenly gave way to river water, four foot deep sand, mud or rough piles of rock and clay.

I owe the whole wonderful trip to my father. My teeth came into my young mouth badly out of place and it was necessary to put on heavy bands. Our Reno dentist arranged to come down to San Francisco and take lessons from an orthodontist in how to straighten teeth so he could do it for several young folk in Reno. He went down for a lesson once a week and then came back and practiced on us! In those days it was all new and extraordinarily painful. I had to leave school for weeks at a time, and my sympathetic father bought both me and himself bikes so we could go riding together. He also promised me that dreamed about bike ride from San Francisco to Los Angeles.

The other members of the party included Professor and Mrs. Nathaniel E. Wilson of Reno, Nevada, and their young, three year old son, Nat, who rode on a special seat on his father's handlebars.   The bycycles of we two young ladies were new models with the first modern-type brakes, but Professor Wilson was due for trouble with his older model, since it had no brakes.

That early morning of June 12, 1894, we two women nervously checked our bikes and luggage for the last time.   We were quite self-consciously aware that we were going on the trip wearing bloomers into an area where many people had never seen either bloomers or women on bycycles before.   But Professor Wilson was calm and collected, as befitted the man of the party, while his little son, Nat, chattered like a blackbird, "When do we go, Daddy?   When do we go?"

At last we were ready.   With a shouted command, "Keep your wheels in the car slots!" Professor Wilson led the way down the smooth cable car slots that led towards South San Francisco, so avoiding the rough cobble stones of those early streets.   Smoothly we glided along the slots through the beautiful, clear and sunny morning, so early that few commuters were up yet.   Our party reached the end of the tracks an hour later, just before the first cable cars were trundled out to begin their "clang-clanging" journey to the City.

Almost from the first our party seemed to get a reception like that of a circus parade!   Horses neighed in astonishment, then often bucked or bolted with their riders or the carriages or wagons they were pulling.   Through the dust clouds churned up from the dry country roads small boys and girls raced like bright-eyed goblins, shouting such pert remarks as "your bloomers are showing!" or the perennial query, "Wherya going?" Stately ladies peered from their carriages, some looking startled, other shocked, a few amused.   Men whose horses were acting up cursed wildly.   Some   youthful ladies who watched were frankly envious, others curled their lips in disdain, while a few laughed hysterically. And everywhere the dogs barked and ran frantically.

In the summer days the heat was too great to ride at midday, so we rested at such times, often under the shade of great oaks or on the verandah of a friendly ranch home, and sometimes at stage stations where the "yip-yip" and whip-cracking of distant stage drivers signaled the rocking approach of the stages. At such times the bees buzzed lazily among the flowers, and the country people, often half or more Spanish, had their siestas. But many would gather around us, asking where we were going and about our machines. The rosy-mouthed and brown-cheeked country children stared and stared until it seemed their eyes would burst!

The first night we passed at San Jose, but the second evening our little party arrived in the warm dusk at the sleepy village of San Juan Bautista, some forty miles south of San Jose, and stayed at the Plaza House. The startled proprietor and his maids kow-towed to us as if we were royalty, and rushed about to prepare delightfully-smelling dishes of crimson and white Spanish foods, or to spread our beds in the guest rooms with the most beautiful old linen. In the morning we were wakened by the deep tolling of the bells of the San Juan Bautista Mission and the sweet scent from the ancient rose gardens.

From San Juan Bautista we pushed our bikes up the steep San Juan Mountains till we would exclaim with joy at the sight of the distant blue Pacific sea. But, when we started down the twisting dirt road on the other side, Professor Wilson's brakeless bike tried with tigerish determination to rush him madly over the cliffs. "The next grade I'll have to do something better than this!" he promised heatedly.

Vinson Brown, age 4, 1916

Dr. and Mrs. Brown's home, Liberty Street, Reno, 1915

Mr. and Mrs. Nathaniel Wilson, with son Nat, accompanied by Miss Bertha Bender, 1894

San Francisco just after the Earthquake in April, 1906, looking down Powell Street from Nob Hill. Hotel St. Francis is large building on middle right, with Union Square just to left of it. (Photograph courtesy of California Historical Society.)

What dust clouds we saw in the Salinas Valley! Giant wagons, pulled by teams of four to twelve horses, lumbered along, carrying crops and lumber to Salinas, each moving with its own rolling cloud of dust from which rang out the loud "gee-haws" and "get up theres!" plus other not so publishable remarks of the drivers, then the whish and snap of the whips.

By evening we were wearily peddling our bikes up the long grade to 1,100 feet high Paraiso Hot Springs in the foothills west of Salinas Valley below the purple shoulders of the Santa Lucia Range.   By this time we were choking and coughing with the dust, while the sweat was hot wetly tickling and trickling down the middle of our backs. But what a picture of paradise was that small but attractive, European-looking hotel at the hot springs! More wonderful still was the sight of steaming hot water in the Paraiso pool.   Into that deliciously warm and fragrant water we soon were to sink, washing off the stains of travel and relaxing aching muscles.

"Schon! Schon! such beautiful ladies!"   exclaimed the jolly German proprietor.   "I vill myself prepare yet the best of everting for you!"   True to his word, he brought out a delicious German meal,   steaming with rich meats and gravies, and himself poured into tall glasses the transplendent claret of a fine wine.

"Really, I cannot drink this!" I protested tactlessly. "My Papa never lets me have alcoholic drinks!"

Such dark clouds appeared on the usually smiling German face.   "But this is my best wine!" he sputtered, his cheeks turning red as fire.

"Bertha!" whispered Mrs. Wilson. "Just pretend to drink it. I will finish for you." She drank my glass indeed, a good Samaritan, and the trick worked fine, bringing back the smiles, except that soon the room began to spin around her and she found it impossible to stand upright!

Piles of loose sand and a hard black adobe clay material, called "hardscrabble" by the natives, made up most of the road the next day, as we peddled laboriously into the upper Salinas Valley.   "Get off your bikes!" cautioned Professor Wilson when we ploughed into four feet deep sand a mile north of the King City Bridge, and had to almost swim through the smothering stuff for two hundred yards!

The Salinas River had few bridges and many times we ladies had to put our feet up on the handlebars in undignified fashion while Professor Wilson took off his shoes and socks so he could push us one at a time through the swirling waters watchful of quicksand. Then, in the middle of the fifth day, we entered the village of San Miguel, famous for its Mission, and ran into pandemonium!

Suddenly we found ourselves in the midst of a religious celebration and procession with everybody dressed in Spanish Californiano costumes.   At the amazing appearance of two ladies in bloomers on bycycles, horses reared, neighed, bucked and rushed off madly in all directions, dogs barked frenziedly, women screamed, little boys and girls rushed in and out yelling like Apaches, and the black eyes of young Senoritas fairly sparked with curiosity.   When the hullabaloo died down, the celebration was forgotten as everybody gathered around to stare and question: "What are those things you wear?"   "Are you women or men?"   "Can you go faster than horses?"   Men from Mars could not have created more curiosity and excitement!

The seventh day saw us laboriously pushing our bikes up the long and winding San Luis grade, a task that took several hours where today cars whisk up the straightaway to the top in a few minutes. . At the top we looked in despair at the steep and twisty road to San Luis Obispo until Professor Wilson suddenly got the brilliant idea of wiring his machine to the other two in tandem fashion so we could use our brakes to hold him and Nat back, as we rushed down the slope.

The ninth day, when we were spiralling down the even more steep and treacherous grade of the Gaviota Pass to the sea near Santa Barbara, Professor Wilson inventively designed still another method of holding his bike back. He tied it, with heavy copper wire, to a large loose fence post, and, dragging this behind him, bumped and lurched his way down the hill. Tired out, we arrived at Santa Barbara at 10 o'clock that night, determined to spend a day of rest and relaxation in that most beautiful city by the sparkling Pacific.

That tenth day we were indeed treated with a royal hospitality worthy of the old Californiano Dons. Graceful girls in colorful Spanish costumes waited on us and our innkeeper surrounded us with good food and happy smiles of welcome. We visited many historic spots and relaxed on the beach or in the lovely cool gardens of the old Mission Santa Barbara, renewing our strength.

What a glory it was to ride the eleventh day on the smooth wet sand along the edge of the ocean eastward toward Ventura! Far to the south stretched the blue Pacific to the hazy shapes of islands in the Santa Barbara Channel, and near at hand the breakers curled in their snow-like crests to sing their lullaby on the sand.

Then, startlingly, racing out of the west, came two other bike riders, young dentists trying to make a biking record from San Francisco to Los Angeles. Alas, they never had a chance to finish their record. The two men, racing at high speed, partly I would guess to impress the ladies present, ran into a pile of kelp in which some large rocks were hidden, and landed, head over heels, sprawled on the beach with broken bikes and bloody noses!

Through roads covered with deep sand and across streams that barred our way, we three riders peddled on toward Los Angeles. One almost tragedy marred this last bit of our journey. In the morning of the twelfth day, at Vijah Station, just beyond Newberry Park, Mrs. Wilson biked hopefully up to a ranch house to ask for milk for her little son, when a large and ugly-looking man rushed from the house, swearing loudly and urging after her an even more ferocious-looking dog. She turned and peddled away furiously, with the dog savagely snapping at her heels, and the man grinning. But the man wiped away the grin when he saw Professor Wilson draw his pistol and take aim to shoot the dog. At that point the dog was called back in a hurry!

After lunch at Calabasas Station, we pushed on over Cahuenga Pass and down into the Los Angeles Plain, reaching the small city (about 56,000 population then) of Los Angeles at 6.45 P.M. after a trip of 515 miles, covered in twelve days, a trip a car does in 9 hours or less today and a jet plane in one hour!

Tired and dusty, we were interviewed and photographed by the newspaper men, and then sought grateful rest at a hotel owned by an aunt and uncle who saw that we had every comfort and were pleased pink to be able to show off such unusual guests!

SAN FRANCISCO AND THE EARTHQUAKE

Many wonderful years in San Francisco I spent before there came the terror of the earthquake and my own "most fantastic story" of what happened to me in that quake, as one man called it.

I was sent down to the "City" to take singing lessons, since my mother insisted I had a better voice than any one she knew and I believe she wanted one of her daughters to be a real singer, as she was herself. Though I did take singing lessons for some time and many people found my voice so sympathetic that it made them cry to hear me, it was not destined that I was to be a singer because the expense of the lessons went up too high and other interests captured my attention.

Soon I found that my family in Reno and also other relatives and friends, kept me busy shopping for them. I was constantly going down to the stores and soon began to learn where the best bargains were and finest materials could be bought. On day my Aunt Eva said:

"Bertha, why don't you become a regular shopper?"

"Why," I exclaimed, "I don't know anything about it! And Clara, my oldest sister, always says I have 'Indian taste' and no style. So I gave up that idea long ago!"

But Aunt Eva kept pushing the idea on me and my increased knowledge of shopping began to give me confidence. When the music professor said I must take three lesson per week, at $5.00 per lesson, I gave up these lessons and went full time into shopping instead.

In a year or two I was grossing over $3,000 per month and learning to guide people from the East on trips through Chinatown. I had learned quite a bit about Chinese Art and soon was taking guests of the different hotels to Chinatown, pointing out to them good buys and bargains as we visited the different exotic shops along Grant Avenue. I even had my own office on Sutter Street over a Snake Drug Store, and how I hated to pass their windows and see those snakes!

The big increase in my business came after I had some cards printed with my name, address and description of my business. I sent these out to everybody I could think of and, as orders came in, I went to see the merchants and arranged to sell on commission for them. I also had great help from my very beloved Uncle Jim Gunn, whose first wife had been my father's cousin, Kate Crocker. As problems came up, he was always ready to lend a helping hand and advice.

My small office on Sutter Street was shared with four girl artists, who had an art collection shop. All this Father considered very wrong at first, as he was raised with the idea that a woman could only be a school teacher or a typist. For a woman to enter business he considered taboo! and felt that he would be criticized about his daughter. But, as my business grew, and more and more people told him how well I was doing, he began to become proud intead of sorry about my work.

At first I had lived with my Uncle Almon and Aunt Eva Bender, but, as soon as I felt myself becoming a business woman I knew the need for greater independence, and so moved into an old brick building that had become a family hotel called the Savoy at the corner of Post and Powell, facing Union Square and catty-corner from the St. Francis Hotel.

A dear old lady, Mrs. Adelaide Haugh, and a neighbor of ours in Reno, came from a trip East and was visiting me at the Savoy Hotel in April, 1906. So she and I were together when the great earthquake came.

A couple of weeks before the earthquake I received notices from many of the stores I traded with to the effect that they were stopping their business with the "shoppers." This was because the privilege had been abused and hundreds were on their books who were using it only to get the discounts for themselves, their families and their friends. The stores had detectives out gathering in the records of the different shoppers. This news shook me to the heart as I was just getting into a fine business and making many wonderful friends. I remember, for example, one customer to whom I sent off an order of six dresses. She kept what she wanted and then called in her friends and sold all the rest. This was a familiar experience in my dealings with such isolated places as Coos Bay, Oregon, where the town in those days had no good highway or railway connections, but was served only by once a week boats and irregular stage coaches.

On receiving the bad news about my business, I, as usual, went to Uncle Jim Gunn for advice, and he said:

"There must be some good reason for the stores' action, and we should go to see them."

The morning of the earthquake we had appointments to see the managers of three stores. Of course we never got there, but I did get a second notice in my mail the day before that I was one of twelve to be kept on their books, since I was getting a good record as a shopper and was having very few returns on my orders. That notice was later burned up on my desk, but it proved two things to my father and sister. It made him realize that I did have a business head, and it proved to Clara that I was beginning to show the good taste   in buying that she never believed I had.

Clara was a wonderful designer of clothes when we were all home together. She didn't need a pattern, but just a piece of cloth and a pair of scissors and some pins. When we were all going to parties we had more dresses than other girls and were the envy of many. Our clothes looked as if they came from the most expensive places in San Francisco in those days.

Many years after the earthquake I was spending the winters in Southern California at the charming Vosburg Hotel in San Jacinto and told my earthquake story to several people. One man said:

"Well, Mrs. Brown, that is the most fantastic story I have ever heard, especially the part about saving everything you owned! It is most hard to believe because I was there myself only two blocks away from where all this happened to you. Everybody lost everything they had and no one could take anything out at any price because the militia had the whole district surrounded and confiscated every sort of conveyance!"

I still insisted my story was true and do to this day. So here is my story:

The night before the earthquake the old lady and I were sitting out in Union Square, watching people going to the Opera where Caruso and other famous singers were giving a performance. A young man friend of mine, Art Baker, spent the evening with us and it was a very warm and sultry evening, earthquake weather! Art was working as an engineer, helping build the tunnels the Southern Pacific Railroad was putting in down near South San Francisco, and it was fortunate indeed that he was interested in me, as you shall hear later!

In the early dawn of April 18, 1906, I woke suddenly

to the feeling of a great power moving me remorselessly. All about me it seemed there was a great roaring, rumbling noise, the sound of things falling, and, then, suddenly, screams. The great force rolled me out of my bed and against the door, which made me realize that I must get that door open quickly, as I had had advice only recently that an earthquake-jammed door couldn't be opened and could trap you inside. So I immediately opened the door and set a chair against it. Then I ran to my old lady friend, Mrs. Haugh, finding her on the floor trying frantically to get dressed. Other shocks followed, shaking us so that it was all but impossible to finish dressing. Not knowing what else to do at the moment, I made her get back into bed and I got in with her. All about us dreadful noises were rising, the fall of parts of buildings crashing into the streets, the groan of timbers and brick under strain, and the screams of people trapped or trying to get out to what they hoped would be safety.

Finally the shakes stopped and we finished dressing. I put on a new green suit and under it a breakfast jacket. The latter I had made mostly by hand, but the back and front had been pleated by a store. I thought it was lovely and so wanted to save it. But, when I went down into Union Square and looked at myself, there were the bright blue pleats hanging below my green suit a good fourteen inches in front and back! However, since many other people were queerly dressed, it did not make much difference.

As it turned out, the only things I lost in the quake were my silver toilet articles that were on my bureau top and became covered with plaster. That happened on my side of the room, but on the other side nothing was covered, as the plaster didn't fall there. In fact it was perfectly extraordinary to us that our whole brick hotel did not collapse around us, as we had been warned that brick buildings were very dangerous in earthquakes. Somehow that building must have been built especially strong because it stood up wonderfully when supposedly much better buildings were collapsing around it!

When we got down into Union Square I discovered that old Mrs. Haugh had really dressed to be warm! She had on a silk suit, a woolen suit and on top of all that a long sealskin coat!   She was dressed for winter instead of a sultry warm morning as it was that day.

For awhile we were both dazed and didn't know what to do except to wait for the civil authorities to take care of us.   A little later I got courage enough to go back into the hotel to get some sandwiches and coffee.   The lobby I found in a terrible wreck, with the heavy counters, desk and chairs all piled up in one end of the big room and the chandeliers twisted off and flung into one corner.   When I came out again, I felt so hopeless because we had only ninety dollars in our purses and that was certainly not enough to buy transportation   anywhere on such a day!

Union Square was, of course, jammed with refugees from the several hotels, including many wealthy people in silks and furs from the St. Francis Hotel and all the stars from the opera that had been playing in the San Francisco Opera House just the night before.   The famous singer, Caruso, was there, and I remembered it astonished me at how excited he was, thinking because he was famous that he would be braver and calmer than the rest of us!

Finally two couples, who lived in the hotel, a Mr. and Mrs. Swinnerton and Uncle John Pew and his wife, asked us to join their party to try to get to Sausalito, which is just north of San Francisco across the Golden

Gate Straits.   Uncle John Pew was head skipper of the
Sausalito Yacht Club and Mr. Swinnerton said he had a
boat to take us across the bay to Marin County where
they had summer homes and also relatives who could
help us.

We took just what we could carry in the way of small
hand-luggage and had to walk down to Kearney and then
down that street to its foot at the bay where Mr. Swinnerton had his private launch. So we started off together
in a group of nine or ten people, all with our hearts in
our throats, and hoping we could make it to the launch.

But, when we reached the middle of Kearney and
started north on that street, the second and third shocks
came, making us feel as if the whole earth had lifted up
beneath us to shake us helplessly like a puppy shakes a
rag doll! It startled us so terribly that dear Mrs. Haugh
got into a panic and I found it impossible to control her.
At the same time, what was my horror to see the very
buildings above us sway outward and almost touch together, blotting out the sky! How dark it became, like
the end of the world!

So many people were screaming and running around
us that we became separated from our party, and there
was nothing left for us to do but to stumble back to
Union Square, often carried along by the rush of the
mob, like chips in a river. There we sat down again
in our helplessness and despair, hoping that at least
the police would sometime find us and help us.

But we hadn't been there too long when I was most
joyful to see our tall young friend, Art Baker, pressing
through the crowd. He first got help and brought our
trunks down the long stairs of the hotel and then over
to where we were sitting on the edge of Post Street in
the square.   Then he made us promise to sit there until he came again.   He had walked about ten miles to

find us and then walked back to the Southern Pacific camp near the tunnels south of the City where he and other engineers and workers were staying.

All the time we were waiting in the square for Art Baker to come, the poor from south of Market were pouring hopelessly up Powell Street towards the hills, with every sort of hand wagon and baby carriage, all loaded to the gills with their pitiful possessions. I remember one woman carrying a parrot on her shoulder and others with bird cages of canaries. Even a monkey hopped up and down on the back pack of one man, and pet dogs and cats were meowing and barking in myriads. This flood of frightened people and animals was a sight I shall never forget!

We sat on our trunks until 3. 30 P. M. and then were overjoyed to see Art coming with a dray wagon pulled by a single big horse. We soon loaded our trunks on the wagon, but everybody was completely astonished that he had reached through to us. Indeed he had been forced to use all his ingenuity and persuasion in reaching us, as the militia were now stopping and confiscating everything on wheels. Not only did he persuade them to let him through because of his promise to us, but he had to be very firm about turning down many offers of hundreds of dollars from people who wanted his help, and was lucky that no one tried to force him with a gun to give up his horse and wagon!

Well, we were the only two people who saved a thing out of that hotel, as it burned down that night when the great fire that had started south of Market Street somehow leaped that huge and wide street and roared up Post Street to Union Square like a thousand lions!

The fire started in a building next to the Emporium Department Store on Market Street. From there it raged east and south before it jumped the street to the north and came thundering up our way. We heard later that the opera stars we first saw in Union Square moved the first night into our Hotel Savoy, which was better preserved than the St. Francis, but then were forced to move out about midnight when word came the fire was fast approaching. They fled in the darkness to some refuge west of Van Ness Avenue, and, if we had stayed, we would have been forced to flee with them.

But all that late afternoon we were driving with Art Baker by a round-about-way first west and then south to the Southern Pacific Camp near South San Francisco. We spent three nights and three days at the camp where two kind fellows gave up their cots to us and all treated us with the utmost respect and care. We sent telegrams to our relatives by any men who said they would be going to telegraph offices. But none of these telegrams ever arrived at my home or reached my relatives.

While at the camp, I sat on the hill top with Art and watched the great fire spreading its devastation through the city. It was like watching clusters of beautiful but terrible red flowers that grew and flickered and sent out dense clouds of smoke over everything. We heard the deep booms of dynamite explosions as the firefighters tried to stop the spread of the flame, but we could see the firelines bending, as the fires leaped over barrier after barrier and even penetrated west of wide Van Ness Avenue in some places. At last, on the third day, the fires began to slacken and retreat.

The third night the men in our camp found out that boats and trains were starting to operate again to carry refugees away from the stricken City. So we were taken, the next day, by the same big dray horse and its wagon down to the Southern Pacific Station and across the Bay. Believe it or not, we got on the very same train for which we already had tickets to Reno!

On our way through San Francisco to the ferry we saw some of the awful destruction of the city by fire and quake, with great piles of blackened rubble and charred timbers. Also we passed dozens of bodies covered with sacks on our way through the south of Market district. It left us with a feeling of sorrow and helplessness that still remains a nightmarish memory.

On the train, we were assigned to the observation car and were astonished to find the opera company all on board! Caruso and all the rest were soon singing away like a bunch of canaries, evidently to keep their voices in good singing condition despite the catastrophe!

At Sacramento I was quite sure no word had reached through to my parents about my safety, so I asked a young man on the train to get in touch with our good friend, Joe Dillman, who was head of the Bell Telephone Company in Sacramento, and tell him to phone my folks. This he did and my family was overjoyed to hear of my safety. When we reached Reno and I rushed out of the train into Father's arms, we all had a big cry! I think I was put to bed in a state of emotional exhaustion and was there for most of a week before I could speak coherently about what had happened to me!

Now I learned what had happened to my family right after the quake. Immediately on hearing the news, my oldest sister had been down to every train that came in in the hope of either finding me or getting some word about what had happened to me. Father was off on one of his driving trips to do some bank business. He drove two horses and had driven all day and up late the night before and was exhausted when he got news of the earthquake. But he immediately hitched up another team to his wagon and started right off for Reno, driving all night long! He had the double concern of worrying about me and also about the banking situation that would arise from the disaster and which he feared would paralyze Reno and all the surrounding cities and towns.

My family heard nothing from me for three terrible days. Knowing I was in a brick building, they were sure that it had collapsed completely. Instead it had been so well-built that it withstood the shock much better than most.

We later learned that two furniture stores across the street from our hotel were destroyed first by their top floors caving in, and one small rooming house, facing the square was completely caved in. Nobody came out alive from that place! If that earthquake had happened three hours later, when most people would have been at work in the office buildings, there would have been far more terrible losses of life.

My oldest sister was planning to be married soon and it was wonderful that I saved much of her wedding trousseau in a large basket trunk I had bought for her. Included was a great deal of the linen the bride usually provided as her dowery in those days.

Father had a rough time in the bank as so many people wanted cash to send to friends and relatives. Many were caught with little cash in their pockets. Fortunately he was able to weather the storm.

I didn't go to San Francisco for over a year, and the first person I located was dear Uncle Jim Gunn, who was in a bank up on Market Street. He was full of courage and determination to make his bank pay, but I could see a great change in his face. It was much older looking. He had lost his original bank on Montgomery Street and his beautiful home on Jackson had been bombed, with only ten minutes notice! In that house he had a pipe organ and thousands invested in records. They only saved their silverware.

Tears were in his eyes as he kissed me goodbye and advised me not to start in business yet with such conditions to fight. I listened to his advice, but my marriage the next year wiped out all possible plans for ever being again a San Francisco business woman.